LIVING WITH DYING

Blessings and Prayers for Those Who Grieve

CONCORDIA PUBLISHING HOUSE · SAINT LOUIS

Copyright © 2012 Concordia Publishing House
3558 S. Jefferson Avenue, St. Louis, MO 63118-3968
1-800-325-3040 · www.cph.org

Scripture quotations are from the ESV Bible® (The Holy Bible, English
Standard Version®), copyright © 2001 by Crossway Bibles, a publishing
ministry of Good News Publishers. Used by permission. All rights reserved.

Hymn texts with the abbreviation *LSB* are from *Lutheran Service Book*,
copyright © 2006 Concordia Publishing House. All rights reserved.

Hymn texts with the abbreviation *TLH* are from *The Lutheran Hymnal*,
copyright © 1941 Concordia Publishing House. All rights reserved.

Hymn 594 © 1991 Robert E. Voelker. Used with permission.

Manufactured in the United States of America

Library of Congress Cataloging-in-Publication Data

Living with dying : blessings and prayers for those who grieve.
        p. cm.
Edited by Scot A. Kinnaman.
Includes indexes.

ISBN 978-0-7586-3404-7

        1. Death--Religious aspects--Christianity--Prayers and
devotions. 2. Bereavement--Religious aspects--Christianity--
Prayers and devotions. 3. Grief--Religious aspects--
Christianity--Prayers and devotions. I. Kinnaman, Scot A.

BV4905.3.L58 2012
242'.4--dc23   2011049459

1 2 3 4 5 6 7 8 9 10   21 20 19 18 17 16 15 14 13 12

Contents

Blessings and Prayers at the Approach of Death

LIVING WITH DYING

The grief you know through the loss of your loved ones may be the most disruptive experience in your life. Grief, with its sense of loss and loneliness, comes with agonizing moments of doubt, fear, questioning, anger—even the feeling of being sick with emptiness and guilt.

There is support for you in your trouble. There is presence of family, friends, and church. There are memories of the past and hope for those who live on. There is, above all, the Lord and Giver of life, who holds you in His arms with comfort, pulls you up when you need support, and helps you endure as you live with your grief.

Blessings and Prayers for Those Who Grieve

You will find in this little book many words that are familiar. The selected Scriptures and hymns have been associated with the Church's ministry of comfort and ultimate hope to those who suffer with the death of a loved one. The devotions and prayers speak to our humanity as we figure out how to navigate the reality of death, whether the death of one we love, or the shadow of death that attends our own lives. In these, too, you will likely hear the echo of Scripture and the themes heard in the Church's worship and in the Sacraments, as these are the chief tools by which the Church does her work. The goal of all this is to bring you the comfort and peace the world cannot give, offer you ways to confront God with your questions and pain, and hear the hope—born and nurtured in faith—of a life beyond death with the God who cared enough to die so that we would not have to die forever.

Scot A. Kinnaman, Editor

Time for Prayer

We appreciate prayer most when we are discouraged. True, the prayer of a believer changes things (James 5:16), but something else also happens: we are changed as God's Word works on our thinking. How wonderful that He has urged us to pray without ceasing!

> But I call to God, and the LORD will save me. Evening and morning and at noon I utter my complaint and moan, and He hears my voice. He redeems my soul in safety from the battle that I wage, for many are arrayed against me. . . . Cast your burden on the LORD, and He will sustain you; He will never permit the righteous to be moved. (Psalm 55:16–18, 22)

We pray because we expect God to hear us. After all, as a part of His invitation for the prayers themselves, He promised to do so. He also promised to carry our burdens for us. Therefore, when in trusting prayer we "let" Him plan and set the best future for us and straighten out the past, our minds are put at ease and our anxieties quieted.

As this is true in sick days, so it is true every day. Prayer is an ongoing conversation with our loving Father. As we pray, His Word reminds us that He is the center of our lives and that His presence means blessings.

We give to God our burdens: sin, worry, loss, heartache, sickness. We also look to Him to supply our needs: forgiveness, increased faith, guidance, strength, relief, healing, patience, peace.

"Evening and morning and at noon I utter my complaint and moan." The assurance that "He hears my voice" will carry you through the long days and through the even longer nights.

The Lord's Prayer

Our Father who art in heaven, hallowed be Thy name, Thy kingdom come, Thy will be done on earth as it is in heaven. Give us this day our daily bread; and forgive us our trespasses as we forgive those who trespass against us; and lead us not into temptation, but deliver us from evil. For Thine is the kingdom and the power and the glory forever and ever. Amen.

MEDITATIONS
and COMFORT

A Christmas Carol

"Christmas will be different this year," said the new widow. Surely it would be; yet it would still be Christmas. It isn't difficult to understand that homes where grief is still fresh will not dive into a world of tinseled madness. But Christmas is more than seasonal decorations, the red and the green, the lights and the tree.

Christmas is the celebration of the most needful event of mankind: the coming of the Savior. Easter, too, may be "different this year," but the significance of the festival hasn't changed. It still means victory. It still heralds resurrection. It still commemorates an emptied grave. For those who mourn, the traditional days of festivity may be different with an emptied chair, but celebrate the festival!

Christmas and Easter can only console, since it is in the incarnation and the resurrection that tears have meaning. And life has enormous meaning also.

Celebrate the festivals, the significance, the importance of the events. Celebrate them at worship. Celebrate them with family. Celebrate them with all the superficialities stripped away. Celebrate them "with the unleavened bread of sincerity and truth" (1 Corinthians 5:8). Therein you will find the Child of the manger, and the Lord of the vacant tomb, and you will find solace for your aches and comfort for your anguish.

Celebrate them as milestones of spiritual growth, rather than memorials to a past that is gone. Remember fondly the good times that earmarked every Christmas and blessed every Easter. But remember also the inspiration, for the gaiety of those times was founded on a remarkable event in Bethlehem and an equally unheard-of happening at a cemetery near Calvary. As you celebrate the festival itself, you will discover God granting you peace as the angels sung of it, and a personal reality that ties your own Good Friday to the Lord's conquest of death. You will experience the truth of the Christian life that begins with birth and sails on past death to resurrection.

The celebrations may be different this year and next, but they will be more meaningful than ever. Without the gimmicks, celebrate the festivals and be enriched beyond your fondest hope. You do have something to sing about.

Blessing in the Sacrament

There's an extra blessing in the celebration of the Lord's Supper many people overlook: In a miraculous way, Holy Communion enacts the mystical fellowship of all the saints on earth and in heaven. Those who have gone before and those who remain are one in Christ's body and blood. In some older church buildings, the Communion rail extended in a half-circle around the altar to symbolize that completeness.

Just listen! You can hear them singing with you—all the heavenly host—the angels of heaven, the saints of ages past, your grandparents or parents or others . . . and your child too. When you commune, you are swept together with them into one great host, rejoicing and praising God and saying, "Hosanna in the highest! Blessed is He who comes in the name of the Lord. Hosanna in the highest!"

What a comfort! What a foretaste of the feast to come!

Evidence of Compassion

I don't go along with those who say it was "God's will" when somebody dies. Death was never God's will or intention for humanity. God says, "I have no pleasure in the death of the wicked" (Ezekiel 33:11). God knows when all people die, but death is the result of our sinful nature. That doesn't mean that some died earlier because they sinned more. The Lord made that very clear in Luke 13.

So to say "God called him home" or "God took him" or "God willed it"—especially as an attempt to rationalize an untimely death—can be misleading language. God permitted life to end, but as the apostle Paul says, "death spread to all men because all sinned" (Romans 5:12).

Compassion is the key note here. Jesus embodied compassion. And we are to evidence it even when we speak of death. Although all suffering, disease, and death ultimately come from our sinfulness, God gives us forgiveness through His Son—and calm in the face of the enemy death.

Still, I understand when some call death "kind

friend" or "sweet" when the mercy of God permits an end to all suffering here. As Revelation 21:4 states, "He will wipe away every tear from their eyes, and death shall be no more, neither shall there be mourning, nor crying, nor pain anymore, for the former things have passed away."

So the victory over death has already been won for you by the life, death, resurrection, and the ascension of Jesus Christ.

4
Suicide

Hope that Transcends

God, we believe in Your tender love for us. Give comfort and strength to those who mourn today. Take away any feeling of guilt and ease the burden of regret. Keep them in Your care and help them to renew their lives in a spirit of trust. We ask this in faith, through Christ, our Lord. Amen.

When the shocking news of suicide enters the life of a believer in Christ, the Christian turns immediately to God and His Word, for only in the eternal love of God can understanding and comfort and strength be found. If God had no message for us in such a time of disaster and grief—if He did not reach out, offering us love and hope—we would be tempted to turn against God and blame Him for the anguish that has come to us.

You can bear the burden of this sorrow if you remember God's word to us in 1 Peter 1:3: "According to His great mercy, He has caused us to be born again to a living hope through the resurrection of Jesus Christ from the dead." When Peter wrote these words, he likely was thinking of how his readers recently had been baptized.

Baptism says God has chosen us, and His door and His arms are open wide to us. He takes us—sinful people that we are—and draws us into the very life and death and resurrection of Jesus. All that Jesus did for us becomes ours in Baptism. He died in our place to pay the penalty for our sins. His death counts for us. Then He rose from the dead, and He shares with us His life with God that doesn't stop at the grave. The new birth in Baptism is birth to a life of hope, because it unites us with Jesus Christ, who rose from the dead. That's why Peter wrote, "He has caused us to be born again to a living hope." That hope transcends this earth and fills all eternity with glory. That hope of salvation belongs to all baptized believers. God's grace is powerful enough and quick enough to forgive each of us who trusts in Christ, regardless of our circumstances. If we didn't believe that, none of us could sleep at night.

Now hear this again: "Blessed be the God and Father of our Lord Jesus Christ!" These words are all the more remarkable because they were originally spoken not in days of sunshine, but in days when the persecuted Church faced darkness, suffering, and anguish. It is a miracle of faith when an afflicted person speaks such words during a time of trouble and uncertainty.

> I walk with Jesus all the way,
>   His guidance never fails me;
> Within His wounds I find a stay
>   When Satan's pow'r assails me;
> And by His footsteps led,
> My path I safely tread.
>   No evil leads my soul astray;
>   I walk with Jesus all the way.
>   (*LSB* 716:5)

5

Assurance

Human Like Me, Jesus

We are tempted to think at times that our Lord was less a man than He is God. That heresy was answered centuries ago; nevertheless there is considerable allegiance to it among contemporary Christians who know better.

When He was tempted, was He *really* tempted, or was it more of an example for us to follow? When He grew weary from the day's preaching and healing, was He *really* tired, or was it merely a compassionate gesture toward the disciples? The questions could go on and on: Did He *really* hunger? Did He *really* need to die? Did He *really* thirst, both at the well and on the cross? Wasn't the one merely an excuse to talk to the sinful Samaritan woman, and the other a ruse to test the mercy of His captors?

And when He cried over Jerusalem and sorrowed over Lazarus, were His tears real? Surely He knew they were wasted over the city, and He would be able to break the latch of death for His friend.

They were *not* crocodile tears, nor was His anger

at the money-changers in the Temple an act. You see, Jesus possessed full humanity. When He took on flesh, He assumed our nature fully. His crucifixion was no mere pantomime to satisfy His enemies' demands. It was genuine. He was real. And He lived life by breathing as we do, by feeling the sharpness of the gravel against His feet, by enduring the sweat of Palestinian heat.

All of this is to say that He fully understands our humanity, for He is human.

We cannot deny His divine nature either—the miracles over nature, over men, and over things underscore that fact fully. He "emptied Himself, by taking the form of a servant, being born in the likeness of men," wrote Paul to the Philippians (2:7). He was and is God, and at His birth He also became fully man.

He wept because sorrow touched Him. He spoke sharply to the Pharisees because they would hear Him in no other way. He fed the thousands because He had compassion on them. And Jesus understands fully what you are experiencing right now. That's why He says, "Come to Me, all who labor and are heavy laden, and I will give you rest. Take My yoke upon you, and learn from Me, for I am gentle and lowly in heart, and you will find rest for your souls.

For My yoke is easy, and My burden is light" (Matthew 11:28–30). Human like us, Jesus knows our needs, and being fully God, He supplies them.

6
Giving Up

I've Had It
....

The temptation to chuck everything comes to those engulfed in the overwhelming tidal wave of grief that follows death. Bitterness is the devil's tool. He will attack when we're least prepared for it. He will dim the vision of the sorrowing so that they fail to see beyond the storm clouds to the bright rays of the distant sun. The devil's objective is suffering, and he will prolong it as much as he can.

There are several ways in which mourners may succumb to his tactics. One is to blame God for the sorrow experienced. Yet sin was not His invention, nor disease. We tend to forget that. As He permits it to occur, so He provides the way of escape, as St. Paul puts it. Remember what he wrote: "No temptation has overtaken you that is not common to man.

God is faithful, and He will not let you be tempted beyond your ability, but with the temptation He will also provide the way of escape, that you may be able to endure it" (1 Corinthians 10:13).

A second tactic the devil employs to add suffering is to urge those who mourn to make hasty decisions while yet in the fog of emotion. Property is quickly disposed of, moves are made to foreign environments, and old supportive patterns of the past are arbitrarily dropped. The trauma of death is complicated by such haste. Proverbs is correct: "A man of quick temper acts foolishly" (14:17).

There are numerous other ways by which sorrowing families and individuals will throw up their hands and exclaim, "I've had it." Embittered by their loss, they make life miserable for others. Or they may sedate themselves by drink or drugs to forget, or by excessive sleeping or even overwork. Unhealthy and unwholesome, these methods are also unsatisfying.

"In due season we will reap, if we do not give up," says the Bible (Galatians 6:9). It has a far more effective way of handling grief. It's called faith. When the temptation is to "chuck everything," to say "I've had it," seek the counsel of the Almighty. He has far better advice for you. "The one who sows to his own flesh will from the flesh reap corruption, but the one who sows to the Spirit will from the Spirit reap eternal life" (Galatians 6:8). That's the kind of wisdom those who mourn need.

7

Comfort

I'm Okay, You're Okay

We accept certain facts about death, without facing up to others. For instance, the Christian sorrows over *his* loss only. When people have become wrapped up in love for each other, the mere thought of an extended separation is saddening. But consider this: separation is not to be forever, *especially* for Christians. Eternity awaits. Reunion is ahead. And recognize this also: for those who die in Christ, life far more glorious than this goes on.

There is no pain. Whether death was preceded by a short or lengthy illness, in the perfection of heaven there can be no disease, no anguish—only joy! The mute speak, the deaf hear, the sightless see, the lame and the frail walk. Wrote St. Paul, "Our citizenship is in heaven, and from it we await a Savior, the Lord Jesus Christ, who will transform our lowly body to be like His glorious body, by the power that enables Him even to subject all things to Himself" (Philippians 3:20–21).

You see, those who die in the Lord are okay! And they would have us know it and feel okay about it, being okay ourselves.

Our Lord's promise of not leaving us desolate is surely another point we must face up to. Through the Holy Spirit our loneliness will be changed into a healthy relationship with Him and the world around us. There is a time when those who mourn must reorient their energies from self-pity, perhaps even guilt, to recognizing that the continuance of normal life faithfully lived is vital to being truly okay.

It may seem a useless exercise, but the point will hit its mark if you in your sorrow admit each time grief wells up, "I'm okay and so is the one I love."

Christ has made it so, and He's more than okay!

Looking for Some Understanding

We may be inclined to entertain hard thoughts against God at times, but we also affirm that He is both kind and faithful. "The Lord is my portion," says the believer in Lamentations (3:24). Though I have lost everything, I have not lost God. Earthly things will pass away, but God lasts forever. "Therefore I will hope in Him," for God is "good to those who wait for Him, to the soul who seeks Him" (3:24–25). We wait for God by faith, and we seek Him in prayer. Though God's reply to us may be long delayed, we wait till it does come.

Here is where the blessed "chain reaction" of Romans 5:3–5 comes in: our suffering produces endurance, and endurance character, and character hope. And this hope "does not put us to shame, because God's love has been poured into our hearts through the Holy Spirit who has been given to us" (v. 5).

Though you are cast down right now, it is but "for a little while" (1 Peter 1:6), that your faith, though tried, may endure. This is so that in being tested, "your faith—more precious than gold that perishes though it is tested by fire—may be found to result in praise and glory and honor at the revelation of Jesus Christ" (1:7).

God's ways are not our ways, nor are His thoughts our thoughts (Isaiah 55:8–9). But His love and compassion for us are sure. "For I know the plans I have for you . . . plans for welfare and not for evil, to give you a future and a hope" (Jeremiah 29:11). We know this is sure because God sent His only Son into the world to suffer and die for our sins.

Of course, that still doesn't stifle all the "why" questions that continue to plague our minds and hearts or the puzzled anger that we may feel at times. I still get angry . . . but I am angry at Death, our fiendish antagonist, not at God.

Listen to the words of a great churchman, Dr. Kent Knutson, whose life was cut short by a rare disease that he contracted on a mission survey trip as president of the American Lutheran Church.

> Death is not to be accepted as much as
> it is to be overcome. . . . I am angry that
> sin and death stalk man—righteous an-
> ger, I pray, that will not be quiet when
> men suffer and die. I am comforted
> only with the knowledge that God is

angry too. So angry that he submitted himself to the same suffering and death and overcame this enemy with his power and gives us the fruits of his victory. He has invited us to share in his death and resurrection. [*Gospel, Church and Mission.* Kent S. Knutson (Minneapolis: Augsburg, 1976), 51]

With that same confidence, your "why" can be changed into "whom." And we can exult with the holy writer, as your eyes turn from ourselves and focus on Christ.

> Let us run with endurance the race that is set before us, looking to Jesus, the founder and perfecter of our faith, who for the joy that was set before Him endured the cross, despising the shame, and is seated at the right hand of the throne of God. (Hebrews 12:1–2)

Your loved one is at the foot of the throne right now, singing hosannas to the heavenly Father with all His other sainted children.

9
Future

Made Beautiful by God
··

The cross on which our Lord gave His life was not at first a thing of beauty, but it is to us now. This ugly instrument of Roman execution has become the very symbol of the Christian faith. Now it is the sign of our hope, our life, and the beauty of our salvation.

Also, a hole in the ground is rarely considered a thing of beauty, much less a rock-hewn tomb. But as you mourn, remember the resplendent beauty of an empty tomb. Its occupant could not be held by the constraints of death. On this day, of all days, remember the beauty of the empty tomb and know that you have not seen the last of your loved one! For as Christ has risen from the dead, so, too, will all who have been buried with Christ in Baptism be raised to life in Christ's resurrection. Yes, despite your tears, you can see the beauty of the grave because you know that the day will come when that grave will be as empty as Christ's was. Through the beauty of Christ's empty grave, death cannot, will not, shall not have the last word today or any other day!

And what of your future, the days and weeks and years ahead that you thought you would experience with your beloved? What will they be like? This much is certain: you are not going into the future alone! God will walk with you to bear you up when your sorrow revisits you in the days ahead. The great Christian apologist C. S. Lewis once said, "God whispers to us in our pleasure, but He shouts to us in our pain." God does not promise that the days will be easy, but He does promise to give you the strength you will need to face each new day. With St. Paul we hear Christ's voice saying, "My grace is sufficient for you, for My power is made perfect in weakness" (2 Corinthians 12:9). Cling to the precious Means of Grace, God's Word and Sacraments, for they alone can strengthen and bring joy even in the face of death and in the hardships of life. Lean on the community of Christ, God's people, who will comfort you and share your burdens as well as your joys. Most important, cling to Christ Jesus, under the shadow of whose cross both life and death have become instruments of His grace.

Mere Breath

....

When you discipline a man with
rebukes for sin, you consume like
a moth what is dear to him; surely
all mankind is a mere breath! *Selah*
"Hear my prayer, O LORD, and give ear
to my cry; hold not Your peace at my
tears! For I am a sojourner with You,
a guest, like all my fathers."

—Psalm 39:11–12

All that Jesus does, He does for us. For us He
prays the Psalms. The Psalms are the prayer book of
Jesus, and one way to read them is from the voice
of Christ. From the cross He cried out the words of
Psalm 22: "My God, My God, why have You forsaken
Me?" Christ is the Suffering Servant, and in Psalm 39
He cries out once again in His suffering. He stood
silent before His accusers, guilty of all the sin of the
world, with the wrath of God upon Him. His life was
nothing more than a breath, a brief sojourn upon
the earth. He was consumed, and He was struck by

the hostility of the punishment as our sin deserved, and it killed Him. The world does not understand this mystery of the cross. In the shameful and humiliating death of Christ is also His glory. Their defeat is secure and eternal, and Christ displays their defeat when He rises on the third day.

All that Jesus does, He does for us. The Christian is baptized into the death of Jesus and raised to a new life in Him. The life of the Christian is not without suffering—indeed, it is permeated with it. But the pain and shame each Christian bears is not empty and without purpose. When Christians put on Christ, they put on His suffering. They, like Him, become suffering servants. Like Him, it is in the pain of the personal cross that the glory of God is revealed. St. Paul writes: "My grace is sufficient for you, for my power is made perfect in weakness. . . . For the sake of Christ, then, I am content with weaknesses, insults, hardships, persecutions, and calamities. For when I am weak, then I am strong" (2 Corinthians 12:9–10). This is the theology of the cross. In weakness, the glory of God is revealed through Christ.

Our suffering, though real and painful, has lost its eternal sting. It has been defeated and destroyed on the cross. Yet, as in Psalm 39, surely all humankind is a mere breath. Our lives appear short. We are sojourners here, and the discipline we receive in suffering can appear fruitless and meaningless. Humankind is mere breath, but on account of Jesus Christ and His death on the cross, this breath is not our own. Our life has been taken up through Baptism into the new life of Christ. We are a new creation made in the image of God. Into our nostrils, He has breathed His own breath. We no longer operate by our own strength. We are no longer alone to trudge through life. In our weakness, the strength of God is revealed. And the strength of God is the cross of Jesus Christ.

11
Assurance

Mindful of His Own

Turn to me and be gracious to me, for I am lonely and afflicted. The troubles of my heart are enlarged; bring me out of my distresses. Consider my affliction and my trouble, and forgive all my sins.

—Psalm 25:16–18

How insignificant I am when compared to the vast universe! Does God really have time for me? He has billions of people to watch over and tens of billions of stars to keep in the appointed course. Why should He be bothered with my aches and worries?

God's Word assures me that He knows my needs and guides me with His strong but gentle hands. I can depend on Him because His faithfulness is firmer than Gibraltar. God's care is so thorough that the failing sparrow and the shooting star are not beyond His notice. Everything moves at His will.

I am more precious to God than sparrows and stars. I am so precious that God bought me back from slavery to sin and death through the blood of His own Son, Jesus, who gave His life for me to cleanse me from sin and give me life never-ending. Because of that redemption, His hands uphold me, and His heart loves me. I am God's child, now and for eternity.

Am I insignificant, frail, lost, worthless? No, for Christ has joined Himself to me, and I cling to Him as only a child can cling. God knows that I am here; God knows that I am in need of help. I know that the Lord loves me; the cross of Jesus tells me of His love. I do not need to be afraid—God cares for me.

Mourning with Hope

If, because of Christ, death is such a blessed event, should Christians mourn?

Dying people instruct their families: "Do not cry for me. Do not be sad." The sentiment is understandable—the dying do not want to hurt their family or make them sad, and they want to give their family confidence that they will be in a better place. But death is sad. It hurts. The trouble with the injunction on crying is that it can make things worse. You feel sad because your friend died, and then you feel sad because you were told not to be.

Death is still our enemy. Even Jesus wept when He heard that His friend Lazarus was dead, and Jesus knew that He would raise Lazarus from the dead. The shortest verse in the Bible tells us about Jesus' tears over death: "Jesus wept" (John 11:35). So should we. We mourn death; we are sad when our loved ones die. There is no shame in our suffering.

But we must remember that death is still defeated. We are not given over to despair. We mourn with joy. We cry with laughter. Our tears are mixed with hope. In the shadow of the grave, we sing of life eternal. In the midst of death, we confess the resurrection. We mourn with hope.

> We do not want you to be uninformed, brothers, about those who are asleep, that you may not grieve as others do who have no hope. For since we believe that Jesus died and rose again, even so, through Jesus, God will bring with Him those who have fallen asleep. (1 Thessalonians 4:13–14)

13
Hope

The Great Hope
of the Resurrection

On the Day of Judgment, the Lord Jesus will return to the earth and call all people out of their graves and give the resurrection to all flesh (believer and unbeliever alike). For the unbeliever, this is a resurrection unto death (in the worst paradox imaginable).

For believers in Christ, this is the resurrection unto life (see John 5:25–29). Just as the soul is set free from the corruption of sin when we die, our bodies are set free from the corruption and bondage of sin in the resurrection. "Our citizenship is in heaven, and from it we await a Savior, the Lord Jesus Christ, who will transform our lowly body to be like His glorious body, by the power that enables Him even to subject all things to Himself" (Philippians 3:20–21).

St. Paul shows us the importance and the great benefits of the resurrection in 1 Corinthians 15 (often referred to as "The Resurrection Chapter"). This chapter gives us comfort in the face of death, the joyous expectation of this corruption putting on incorruption and our mortality putting on immortality.

> So is it with the resurrection of the dead. What is sown is perishable; what is raised is imperishable. It is sown in dishonor; it is raised in glory. It is sown in weakness; it is raised in power. It is sown a natural body; it is raised a spiritual body. If there is a natural body, there is also a spiritual body. Thus it is written, "The first man Adam became a living being"; the last Adam became a life-giving spirit. But it is not the

spiritual that is first but the natural, and then the spiritual. The first man was from the earth, a man of dust; the second man is from heaven. As was the man of dust, so also are those who are of the dust, and as is the man of heaven, so also are those who are of heaven. Just as we have borne the image of the man of dust, we shall also bear the image of the man of heaven. (1 Corinthians 15:42–49)

After the resurrection, the Scriptures tell us about the "new heavens and a new earth." "But according to His promise we are waiting for new heavens and a new earth in which righteousness dwells" (2 Peter 3:13; see also 1 John 3:2–3; Revelation 21:1–8). This promise is the solid foundation of our faith and hope. We will dwell there eternally in the face of our Savior, Jesus (Revelation 22:4), because He, in His mercy and love and in His suffering and blood, has declared us to be righteous and holy.

If it were left to us to fight against death, we would have no hope, no chance. By our own efforts we cannot dispel the gloom of the grave. Through our own works we cannot escape the sting of death, sin, or the judgment that is to follow. But praise be to our Lord Jesus Christ who has done the work for us, died in our place, carried our condemnation, and forgiven our sins. Because our Jesus has taken up the fight against death and won, we live and die with a full confidence that we are the Lord's. He has for us the gift of the resurrection of the body and life everlasting.

Strength

Soaring with the Everlasting God

Have you ever watched an eagle soar? It's a beautiful sight. If you pay careful attention, the eagle's flight is quite instructive. Eagles are powerful birds, yet they don't soar by the power of their wings. They are able to soar because of the current of the wind. That's why they don't get tired; they aren't relying on their strength, their resources. If they did, they would grow weary and fall to the ground. Instead, they rely on the wind currents to keep them aloft. In the same way, God wants us to rely on Him and His Spirit so that we can soar, not only in this life but also in the life that is to come. He wants us to soar with Him, the everlasting God.

Isaiah wrote, "Why do you say, O Jacob, and speak, O Israel, 'My way is hidden from the LORD, and my right is disregarded by my God'?" (40:27). It's so easy at a time such as this to think that either the Lord doesn't know what's going on in your life or He simply doesn't care. We know that is not the case, even while we can't explain why such tragedies happen.

15
Resurrection

The Lord Knows
the Hurt of His People

What we do know is this: the Lord is not unaware of you or your sorrow. He is not uncaring. He cries every tear with you. Who would know better than our heavenly Father what it is like to lose a beloved Son? He sent His own Son into this sinful world, knowing what that would mean. There was no other way for sinners such as you and me to be rescued from eternal destruction. We needed a sinless Substitute. Yet no one but God Himself is without sin in this creation ruined by the disobedience of Adam and Eve. Thus out of His great love for us, God sent forth His beloved and only Son to our world. The Son of God humbled Himself, and by the power of the Holy Spirit was planted as a seed in the womb of a virgin. He was born of a human mother, Mary, and like us was subject to God's perfect Law. But unlike us, Jesus obeyed the Law perfectly so that He might redeem us from the curse of the Law. Sin's curse brings death. Jesus willingly took your curse and mine to that accursed tree of the cross and died there to take death away forever.

Did the Father not know what was happening? Didn't He care? Of course He knew and cared excruciatingly. Then why did He do it? If we didn't have a sinless Substitute, then death would have won, and the continuation of life here in this world would have been pointless. God gave His beloved Son to death because He loved us and wanted us to have life with Him now and forever.

But that's not all. Three days later, our heavenly Father raised Jesus from the grave, for death could not hold Him. Now He promises us, and all who believe in His Son, that those who are joined with Him by faith are heirs of the same resurrection, the same hope, the same new and eternal life that Jesus has. All of this is guaranteed by the resurrection of Jesus Christ. Because of Christ's resurrection, we can rejoice in the resurrection of the dead and the life of the world to come.

16
Trust

Facing the Future

The question remains: "How do we go on from here? Where will we find the strength?" Our strength is not found within ourselves or our own resolve or determination to continue with life. Instead, God says, "Lift up your eyes on high and see. . . . The Lord is the everlasting God, the Creator of the ends of the earth. . . . He gives power to the faint, and to him who has no might He increases strength. . . . They who wait for the Lord shall renew their strength; they shall mount up with wings like eagles; they shall run and not be weary; they shall walk and not faint" (Isaiah 40:26, 28, 29, 31).

If you have been given faith, then you have also been given wings! So spread your wings, and know that the Lord lifts you in His hands. Don't depend on your own resources. Trust His good and gracious will for you! Believe Him! Soar! Sail on the wind that the Spirit provides in His Word, and you will not grow weary, you will not be faint. Those who hope in the Lord will renew their strength as they soar with our everlasting God.

17
Children

The Kingdom Belongs to Children, Now and Forever

> Jesus said, "Let the little children come to Me and do not hinder them, for to such belongs the kingdom of heaven."
>
> —Matthew 19:14

These words are spoken not only now, at the passing of your child, but they were spoken at the birth of your child. That is, they were spoken at your child's new birth by water and the Spirit. As part of the baptismal service, these words remind us that children, though they do not have the maturity of adults, are received by our Lord Jesus. In Baptism, your child received the kingdom of heaven. Jesus' words are a promise to you that even now your child is with Jesus in heaven.

In fact, Jesus' words tell us that not only are children received by Him, but children also are those to whom heaven belongs. Just as the weak in Christ are strong and the poor are rich, so also the children are the faithful ones. In this account Jesus teaches us not to keep children from His presence, from hearing His Word. Even as you brought your child to be baptized, to worship, and even to the altar with you, you brought your child to Jesus. Your child was a faithful one.

Your child now lives with Jesus, yet you remain here in sorrow. But Jesus is also with you here. Even as you long for fellowship with your child, Jesus, who binds us to one another on earth, also binds us to those with Him in heaven. Christians are not separated into those in heaven and those on earth. Rather, all who are baptized into Christ have received forgiveness of sins and are united as the Church, His saints, whether in heaven or on earth. Wherever Jesus is, there are His saints.

Even as Christ rules in heaven, He also lives as

your friend here. Jesus takes on your burdens and gives you the blessings of heaven. He mourns with you as you mourn your child, and as you partake of His body and blood. He strengthens your fellowship with Himself and with your child. At the altar of God, you are as close to your child as ever, for your child worships at the heavenly altar even as you worship at the earthly one. Nothing can separate you from the love of Christ; nothing can separate you from this spiritual fellowship with your child. Even if for a little while you cannot hold your child in your arms, you are both held in the arms of your Savior. Your fellowship remains forever in the Lamb.

18
Guilt

The Scapegoat

The word *if* is small in size, but powerful in impact.

It's a word used often in self-punishment. "*If* I had done this, such-and-such would never have happened." "*If* I had only checked on it sooner." "*If*" can become a diabolical evil. We are tempted to use it against others also. "Lord, if You had been here, my brother would not have died" (John 11:21).

The search for scapegoats is not a new device at all. The ancients actually took a goat and pushed it over a cliff as a symbol of atonement. The goat was loaded with the sins of the people, taking their place, and earning forgiveness for them. Job despised all of the evils that befell him, and came through his grief with the awareness that a divine Scapegoat would rescue him. He exclaimed, "For I know that my Redeemer lives, and at the last He will stand upon the earth" (Job 19:25). St. Peter identified the divine Scapegoat when he wrote, "He Himself bore our sins in His body on the tree, that we might die to sin and live to righteousness" (1 Peter 2:24).

For us the coming of Christ is no "iffy" question. It was to love us into eternity, and the price was His sinless life, which He gave willingly. Through Him we experience redemption, forgiveness. There is no "if" about that either, unless it is "if we believe."

To permit that small word to become such a massive burden, such a dictatorial influence, is to flail the mind and the body needlessly. To regard the death over which you sorrow only in terms of "if" is to miss finding the only Scapegoat that matters:

Jesus Christ. Martha's accusation was answered with compassion from Christ. Lazarus was called forth from the grave to a new life. "I am the resurrection and the life," said Jesus. "Whoever believes in Me, though he die, yet shall he live, and everyone who lives and believes in Me shall never die" (John 11:25b–26).

Then He asked Martha a very important question: "Do you believe this?"

She put all the "ifs" aside and exclaimed, "Yes, Lord; I believe that You are the Christ, the Son of God, who is coming into the world."

That's the way to deal with satanic "ifs." Faith!

19
Comfort

To Meditate upon Death Is Life

O devout soul, keep Christ, your blessed Savior, always in mind and you will not fear the terror of death. If the violence of death grieves you, let the mighty power of Christ Your Lord comfort you. The Israelites could not drink water from Marah because of its bitterness, until the Lord showed Moses a tree, which "He threw . . . into the water, and the water became sweet" (Exodus 15:25). If you dread the bitterness of death, do not be afraid, because God shows you a tree, which converts its bitterness into sweetness, that is, the Branch that sprung from the root of Jesse (Isaiah 11:1). That Branch is Christ who says, "If anyone keeps My word, he will never see death" (John 8:51). Our life here is full of burdens. It is, therefore, a blessing to find any comfort and alleviation of its misery. After all, it is not the Christian himself, but only his troubles that die. This departure of the soul that we think of as death is not an exit but a transition. We don't lose our departed loved ones; we simply send them on before us. They do not die, but arise into a higher life. They do not forsake us, they are not forever parted from us, they just precede us, into glory. They are not lost to us, rather only separated for a time. When the Christian dies, it is to live a new life. And while we in tears place his or her body in the grave, he or she rejoices in the unspeakable gains of life in glory.

Our friends and loved ones die. In truth this means they cease sinning, and all their anxiety, their struggles, and their misery also cease. They die in the faith. This means they depart from what is only a shadow of life here and pass through to true life; out of the darkness and mystery of this world into the light of heaven; from the temporary life with men, to dwell forever with God.

Life is a voyage over a troubled sea. Death is the port of safety for which we are bound. Therefore, we should not grieve that our loved ones have died, but we should be glad for them since they have come through the stormy sea to their port of eternal rest. This life is a long and weary imprisonment for the soul, and death is its liberation. For this reason, old Simeon, about to die, exclaimed, "Lord, now You are letting Your servant depart in peace" (Luke 2:29). He desired to be allowed to depart as if he was here confined in a bodily prison. Let us be glad for our loved ones, since they have been released from this prison and have attained to true freedom. So also, the apostle prays to be released and be with Christ (Philippians 1:23), as if in the earthly body he has been bound in some sort of miserable slavery. Shall we put on mourning clothes for them when they have been clothed in the white robes of the redeemed (Revelation 7:9)? . . . Shall we vex ourselves with tears and groans for them, or add more sadness to our lives when "the Lord GOD will wipe away tears from all faces" and for them "death shall be no more, neither shall there be mourning, nor crying, nor pain anymore, for the former things have passed away" (Isaiah 25:8; Revelation 21:4), and they "rest from their labors" (Revelation 14:13)? Shall their departure plunge us into excessive sadness, when they, in the company of the angels of God, are exulting in true and lasting joy? Shall we lift up a weeping voice for them when they sing a new song in the presence of the Lamb, having harps and golden bowls (Revelation 5:8–9)? Shall we grieve that they have departed from this world, when their departure is a matter of such joy and blessing for them?

Christ Himself shows us how great a blessing it is for one to exit this world: when His disciples were saddened because He had told them He was about to leave them, He replied, "If you loved Me, you would have rejoiced, because I am going to the Father, for the Father is greater than I" (John 14:28). Suppose you were sailing in a raging storm with the wind pummeling your ship and stirring up the waves against you, and every moment you were threatened with destruction, would you not be looking for the safety of a port with all possible speed? Behold, the world is tottering and wavering to its fall, and not only its old age testifies to its impending ruin, but also by the sign that the "end of all things is at hand" (1 Peter 4:7). And do you not thank God, and will you not be glad, that your loved ones are now safe with God, having been spared and delivered from that awful ruin and shipwreck, and the imminent plagues that so threaten our world with destruction? In whose hands can the salvation of your departed be safer than in the hands of Christ? Where can their soul abide more securely than in the heavenly kingdom?

Hear the holy apostle who says concerning death: "To die is gain" (Philippians 1:21). It is gain to have escaped from the increasing burden of sin! It is gain to have fled the distressing evils that afflict us. It is gain to have passed through into the possession of the better things that God has laid up for those who love Him.

If those whom you have lost through death were very dear to you, let God, who was pleased to take them to Himself in glory, be dearer. Do not be angry with the Lord, for He has taken nothing away except what He has given—He has simply taken His own, He has not taken yours away (Job 1:21). Do not be angry with the Lord for taking back again what He had simply entrusted as a loan. The Lord alone sees the approaching evils and He lovingly chose to take your loved one away from the adversity He saw coming. . . .

If you have lost dear ones through death, believe that you will be with them again and they will be dearer than before. For a brief time they are separated from you, but for a blessed and unending eternity you will be reunited to them. We hold the sure and certain hope that we, too, will depart this life, as some of our dear ones already have—those we have sent before us—and we shall come to that life where those loved ones will be better known and better loved than we ever loved them here. We will love them without any fear of anything marring our perfect love.

No matter how many souls there will be and how many there have already been, still the great assembly in heaven will receive our souls with joy. There, with boundless joy, we will be permitted to recognize the faces of those whom we have loved and lost. We will be able to converse with them through eternity. There, the sister will walk hand-in-hand with her brother, and children with parents. No evening will interrupt the glad festivities of that eternal day.

Therefore, do not dwell so much upon the time of your loved ones' departure, but rather upon the glad time of reunion, when they will actually be restored to you on the morning of the resurrection

(Acts 3:20). When our faith in the resurrection is strong and firm, death loses much of its terror, and we look upon it rather as a quiet sleep. We may find hints of the resurrection in nature. The sun daily sets to then usher in the splendor of a new day. The plant that lies dead through the long winter springs to new life at the approach of spring. The fabled phoenix produces itself again in death. As the seasons end, they begin again, keeping up a constant succession. Fruit matures and dies to reproduce other fruit from its seed—unless the seed first decays and dies, it will not spring up with new fruit. So it is that in nature all things are perpetuated by dying; out of this counting cycle of death comes new life. Shall we suppose that God has no purpose in placing such types before us in nature? Do we hold nature in these natural resurrections to be more powerful than God who promises to raise our bodies on the Last Day? He who gives life to dead and putrid seeds (1 Corinthians 15:37), so that they produce food for your life here, will, to a greater extent, raise you and yours from the dead so that you will live with them in eternity. God has called your beloved ones to their own beds (Isaiah 57:2). Do not, I beg, begrudge them this holy rest. In but a little while they shall rise again.

Perhaps it was your hope that your loved ones [before their death] would be useful members of the Church Militant here on earth; but it has pleased God for them to be members of the Church Triumphant. Let what pleases God also please you. Perhaps it was your hope that your loved one would acquire knowledge of many things [before departing]; but it pleased God that they learn true wisdom in the heavenly school. This pleased God; let it also please you. Perhaps it was your fond hope that before death your loved ones would be raised from the dust and be made to sit with princes (Psalms 113:8); but it pleased God for them to put them in company with the princes of heaven, even the holy angels. This pleased God, so oh, let it also please you. Perhaps it was your hope for them to acquire great wealth; but it pleased God that instead of this they should come into possession of the inconceivable delights of the heavenly kingdom. This pleased God; let it also please you.

O righteous God, You have given and You have taken away; blessed be the name of the Lord (Job 1:21).

Children

Treasure Island

....

A lawyer once pointed out to me that though I may not have vast holdings, my greatest treasure is my children; thus I should designate in my will who should care for them in the event of our death, as my wife and I did. We may agree with the poet that "no man is an island," yet we cannot help but see an individual with whom we would like to commune as an island of treasures.

Children are both "Treasure Islands" and treasured ones, for within their very beings God has put a bit of Himself, a little of the glory of heaven reflected in their eyes, something of His mystery, and much of His love. We celebrate their arrival and grow warm in the worn ruts of their growth. The psalmist has captured the thought well when he exults, "Behold, children are a heritage from the Lord, the fruit of the womb a reward" (Psalm 127:3).

It is when a child, so fresh a flower, so promising a one, is called from our parental arms to those of Him who is Parent to us all that the treasure's real value is realized. The Pauline concept of having "this treasure in jars of clay" is clearly relevant. The frailty of bone and sinew, of heart and brain, is all too much to face, yet face it we must—but in a context where the child belongs to God and is shared with us.

Christ's love of little children is a classic truth. "Let the little children come," He said when the disciples sought to prevent them (Matthew 19:14). He treasures their faithfulness and points to them as examples for us, even at the time of tragic loss: "Unless you turn and become like children, you will never enter the kingdom of heaven. Whoever humbles himself like this child is the greatest in the kingdom of heaven" (Matthew 18:3–4). Surely He who gave them life now grants them a dividend exceeding that of men, for He treasures children even more than we who are their earthly parents.

Our Lord was touched deeply by the death of youngsters. The Gospels tell us He called them to life: Jairus's daughter (Mark 5:21–24, 35–43), and the son of the widow of Nain (Luke 7:11–17). These treasured islands were separated from Him and life no longer. It is so even now.

Unrealized Deliverances

Then God opened her eyes, and she
saw a well of water. And she went
and filled the skin with water and
gave the boy a drink.

—Genesis 21:19

The well had been there all the while, in plain
sight. Still Hagar had not seen it.

Abraham had realized that Hagar and her son,
Ishmael, could no longer stay in his camp without
strife, now that Isaac had been born to Sarah, his
wife. So he had given Hagar supplies of food and
water and had bidden her and her son go. Hagar had
become lost in the wilderness, had used up her drink-
ing water, and in despair prepared to die. She believed
God had forgotten her despite His promise to make of
her son a great nation. She wept hopelessly, but God
heard her weeping and, opening her eyes, caused her
to see the well that had been there all the while.

Neither does God forsake us. We sometimes fear
that He has forsaken us too. But He cannot forsake

us. He has given His promise concerning us and will keep it as surely as He kept it to Hagar and her son. Still we sometimes cry, "Where is His help?"

It is not because His help is not there that we do not see it. It is because our eyes, like Hagar's, are blinded by grief, hopelessness, unbelief.

Many of us have already experienced God's unexpected help, God's unexpected solution of our troubles or the troubles of our loved ones. Later we realize that it was there all the while, waiting, perhaps even visible, had we eyes of faith to see it.

One thing we can depend on is this: God knows our needs even better than we do; indeed, even before we do. Therefore when the need arises, the help will be there.

22
Grief

You Don't Understand—
A Conversation

Then God formed man of the dust of the ground, breathed into his nostrils the breath of life, and man became a living being.

Therefore as sin came into the world through one man and death through sin, and so death spread to all men because all men sinned.

Life from God.

Death from sin.

I'm not sure I want to talk about it.

What are you afraid of?

I don't want to talk about that either.

Are you afraid of God?

That's absurd.

You could hide in the bushes with Adam and Eve.

You don't understand.

I certainly do not understand.

I don't understand it either.

How do you feel?

It hurts and I'd rather not talk about it.

Is it the finality of it all? The pain of loss?

Yes, both, and neither, but I don't want to talk about it.

Sometimes it's better to talk about those things.

Sometimes it takes more time and less talk.

You know you can tell me anything.

If I had something to say you'd be the first to hear.

You know I love you.

(Silence)

You know God loves you and will help you

through the pain and loss.

(Silence)

Maybe we don't need to talk about it right now.

(Silence)

(Silence)

23
Children

Your Child Is with the Lord

> [David] said, "While the child was still alive, I fasted and wept, for I said, 'Who knows whether the LORD will be gracious to me, that the child may live?' But now he is dead. Why should I fast? Can I bring him back again? I shall go to him, but he will not return to me."
>
> —2 Samuel 12:22–23

It seems the most terrible of injustices that a baby, barely knit together in the womb, should die. For those who have lived to age 70 or more, we say, "At least she lived to a good old age." Even when young people die, we have memories of the games they played or the work they did. We knew them as individuals. Why does God take the helpless and leave those who are practiced in their sin? Why does He let parents outlive children?

We should know that your baby is not in pain or suffering. We may share David's hope that his uncircumcised newborn infant is with the Lord (2 Samuel 12:23). We, like David, know that God is a God of mercy and loving-kindness. He binds us to Baptism as the Means of Grace appropriate for bringing faith and forgiveness to infants, but God may have a method that He does not reveal to us whereby He works faith in infants of the faithful who for some reason could not be baptized. Because we do not know, we should not neglect baptizing infants. God's will is always for the best, and we do know that it is the will of our Savior, Jesus, to receive even infants (Luke 18:15).

Indeed, your baby is not suffering. Could there be anything better for your child than to be knit together according to the Lord's handiwork and then to be received into His eternal kingdom? We on this earth have months or years of toil and hardship yet to endure, and we see Jesus only by faith. We may hope your child sees Him now, face-to-face, that your child is comforted now, even if we are not fully.

Our Lord Jesus Christ does remain with us to comfort us in our sorrow. He was conceived and knit together in Mary's womb, born as an infant to redeem even infants, and suffered on the cross to receive into Himself the suffering of all people. He receives your sorrow now and unites you to Himself—and, we may presume, to your baby—when you gather with all the company of heaven in the worship of the Church and sing "Holy, Holy, Holy" and eat and drink His body and blood. Our Lord is with you even as He prepares a place for you and promises you, "Let the little children come to Me and do not hinder them, for to such belongs the kingdom of heaven" (Matthew 19:14).

24
Trust

Crying Out to God

[Jonah prayed]: "I called out to the LORD, out of my distress, and He answered me; out of the belly of Sheol I cried, and You heard my voice."

—Jonah 2:2

We should cry out to God in such a way that we're convinced in our heart that He will answer. It should be a cry that allows us to boast, as Jonah did, that God answers when we cry out in our need. This is simply crying out with the heart's true voice of faith. Unless we first lift up our hearts to God, we are unable to lift up our heads or hold up our hands.

With the help and support of the Spirit, we run to an angry God, looking for His undeserved kindness in the middle of His anger. When we lift our heart in this way, we willingly endure punishment from God and we continue to look for His mercy. Notice what strong character such a heart must have. Though surrounded by God's anger and punishment, it doesn't seem to be aware of them. Instead it sees and feels only God's kindness and mercy. Though the heart is clearly aware of God's anger and punishment, it simply doesn't want to see or feel them. Rather, it's determined to look for God's kindness and mercy—no matter how hidden they might be.

Turning to God is difficult. Breaking through His anger, punishment, and displeasure is like running through a row of thorns or even through a line of spears and swords. It's only with a sincere cry of faith that we can break through. When we cry out in this way, we know in our heart that God hears us.

Eternal Life Begins Now

···

Truly, truly, I say to you, whoever believes has eternal life.

—John 6:47

One could preach a hundred thousand years about these words and emphasize them again and again. Yes, one can't speak enough about it. Here, Christ explicitly promises eternal life to the believer. He doesn't say that if you believe in Him you will have eternal life. Rather He says that as soon as you believe in Him you already have eternal life. He doesn't speak of future gifts but of present ones. He is saying, "If you believe in Me, you are saved. You already have eternal life."

This passage is the cornerstone of our justification. With it, we can settle the disputes we're having about how we receive God's approval. Good works don't lead us to heaven or help us in the sight of God. Only faith can do this. Of course, you should do good works and live a holy life in obedience to God. But these efforts won't help you earn salvation. You already have eternal life. If you don't receive it while here on earth, you'll never receive it after you leave. Eternal life must be attained and received in this body.

Yet how does a person acquire eternal life? God becomes your teacher, for He tells you about eternal life through those who preach His Word. He convinces you that you should accept His Word and believe in Him. This is how it begins. Those same words that you hear and believe will lead you to none other than the person of Christ, born of the virgin Mary. God will take you nowhere else. If you believe in Christ and cling to Him, you are redeemed from both physical and spiritual death. You already have eternal life.

26
Comfort

In Need of Comfort

I will never again curse the ground because of man, for the intention of man's heart is evil from his youth. Neither will I ever again strike down every living creature as I have done.

—Genesis 8:21

God is speaking here as if He were sorry that He had punished the earth because of humans. It almost sounds as if He is criticizing Himself for dealing so harshly with the world. We shouldn't take this as meaning that God changed His mind about His creation. Instead, we should take comfort from this passage. God, in effect, blames Himself in order to encourage and lift the spirits of His little flock. He tells His people that He wants to be merciful from this point on.

Noah and his family needed comfort. They were terrified by God's anger, which had just destroyed the world. Because their faith was shaken, God wanted to show Himself in a way that would make them expect nothing else but His good will and mercy. So He was present at their sacrifice, talked to them, and told them He was pleased with them. He told them that He was displeased about destroying the human race and promised never to do it again. God wasn't being inconsistent or changing. No, He wanted these people, who were witnesses of the effects of His anger, to change their attitudes and perceptions of Him.

People who are going through spiritual trials know how important it is to hear words of comfort. They need to be told to hope in God's good will and dismiss discouraging thoughts of impending doom.

A whole day, even an entire month, may not be enough time to comfort them. Recovery from sickness often takes a long time. In the same way, wounded hearts can't be quickly healed with one little word. Because God is aware of this, He uses a variety of ways to show people His good will and mercy—even blaming Himself.

27
Assurance

Victory through Death

Since therefore the children share in flesh and blood, He Himself likewise partook of the same things, that through death He might destroy the one who has the power of death, that is, the devil.

—Hebrews 2:14

We must have the kind of Savior who can save us from the power of this world's god (2 Corinthians 4:4), and this world's ruler (John 16:11), the devil.

We must have a Savior who can save us from the power of sin and death. Christ must be the true, eternal God, through whom all believers receive God's approval and are saved. If Christ weren't greater or better than Moses, Elijah, Isaiah, or John the Baptist, then He wouldn't have been able to reclaim us. Because He is God's Son, He was able to reclaim us and free us from our sins when He shed His blood. If we believe this, we can rub it in the devil's face whenever he tries to torment or terrify us with our sins. This will quickly defeat the devil. He will be forced to retreat and leave us alone.

Here's an illustration that can help us understand how Christ defeated the devil by dying. The fishing hook, which is Christ's divinity, was concealed by the earthworm, which is Christ's humanity. The devil swallowed both when Christ died and was buried. But Christ's divinity ripped open the devil's stomach so that it couldn't hold Christ anymore. The devil had to throw Him up. The devil ate something that proved to be fatal. This truth gives us wonderful comfort. Just as the devil couldn't hold on to Christ in death, so the devil can't hold on to us who believe in Christ.

LIFE,
DEATH,
and THE RESURRECTION

For the wages of sin is death, but
the free gift of God is eternal life in
Christ Jesus our Lord.

—Romans 6:23

The Cause of Death

Death was not part of God's original creation. In the first chapter of Genesis, we hear the wonderful refrains "It was good" and "It was very good." Life was flourishing! Death was not part of God's good creation.

How, then, did death begin? After God created Adam and Eve, He placed them in the Garden of Eden and gave them "dominion over the fish of the sea and over the birds of the heavens and over every living thing that moves on the earth" (Genesis 1:28). In the midst of the garden, God planted the tree of life and the tree of the knowledge of good and evil. God commanded Adam and Eve: "You may surely eat of every tree of the garden, but of the tree of the knowledge of good and evil you shall not eat, for in the day that you eat of it you shall surely die" (Genesis 2:16–17). Tempted by Satan to doubt God's Word and to desire what was forbidden them, Adam and Eve sinned by eating from the forbidden tree. Because Adam listened to Eve and ate of the tree that God had commanded him not to eat, Adam, and all humankind after him, is cursed to labor for the bread he eats "till you return to the ground, for out of it you were taken; for you are dust, and to dust you shall return" (Genesis 3:19). The Scriptures go on to record,

> Then the Lord God said, "Behold, the man has become like one of Us in knowing good and evil. Now, lest he reach out his hand and take also of the tree of life and eat, and live forever—" therefore the Lord God sent him out from the garden of Eden to work the ground from which he was taken. He drove out the man, and at the east of the garden of Eden He placed the cherubim and a flaming sword that turned every way to guard the way to the tree of life. (Genesis 3:22–28)

Every human being born since, every one a descendant of Adam, has an inheritance of sin and death. Each of us is a sinner. Each of us, then, will die. Death is the judgment for our sin, as Scripture tells us: "The wages of sin is death" (Romans 6:23; see also James 1:15). This is why death is such a fearful thing. It is the punishment for our sin, and on the other side of death, we face condemnation and judgment for our sin.

> Sin came into the world through one man, and death through sin, and so death spread to all men because all sinned. (Romans 5:12)

There is nothing that we can do to eliminate death. There is no human accomplishment, effort, or ingenuity that can beat back death and give man immortality. Until the Lord returns, every single person will die. We all need a Savior to rescue us from death.

> "O death, where is your victory?
> O death, where is your sting?"

> The sting of death is sin, and the power of sin is the law. But thanks be to God, who gives us the victory through our Lord Jesus Christ.
> (1 Corinthians 15:55–57)

The Death of Jesus

Death has a claim on all of us because of our sin. But Jesus had no sin, and so the grave had no claim on Him. Death went too far when it took hold of Jesus, and death lost its claim on all humanity. Death is destroyed. Jesus takes upon Himself our death, the punishment for our sins, the condemnation that we deserve, and the wrath of God that our sin had kindled. He took it on Himself so that our death no longer forever separates us from God. The Lord gives us salvation in the place of condemnation and forgiveness in the place of judgment—life in the place of death.

We still experience death, but we now have new life in Christ. And the life we now live is freed from the fear of our own death, because in Jesus we know that death is not the last word. We have this explained beautifully in Hebrews:

> Since therefore the children share in flesh and blood [we have mortal bodies], [Jesus] Himself likewise partook of the same things [in His incarnation, taking on our humanity], that through death He might destroy the one who has the power of death, that

is, the devil, and deliver all those who
through fear of death were subject to
lifelong slavery. (Hebrews 2:14–15)

All of this is manifest before the world in the
Lord's resurrection. When He came out of the grave
on the third day, the reign of death ended. Before the
resurrection, the grave could have been marked with
a sign: "One Way—No Way Out." But Jesus turns
and walks out of the grave. He makes a way through
death. Jesus' resurrection proves that death's grip is
broken, that the grave is not the end, and that all
flesh will rise on the Last Day.

In the death and resurrection of our Lord Jesus,
we have the fulfillment of this great promise:

And He will swallow up on this moun-
tain the covering that is cast over all
peoples, the veil that is spread over all
nations. He will swallow up death forever; and the Lord God will wipe away
tears from all faces, and the reproach
of His people He will take away from
all the earth, for the Lord has spoken.
It will be said on that day, "Behold,
this is our God; we have waited for
Him, that He might save us. This is the

LORD; we have waited for Him; let us be glad and rejoice in His salvation." (Isaiah 25:7–9)

The Christian's Death

Death is our enemy, but it is our destroyed enemy. This understanding, this paradox, determines our attitude, as Christians, toward dying. Like Jesus, we do not simply accept death as something good or natural or inevitable. We do not need to "come to grips" with dying, with being sick, or with getting old. Death is and will remain our enemy. But because of Jesus' death, we realize that death has no power over us, that the grave is nothing to fear, that all the darkness of the tomb has been replaced by the radiance of Jesus' resurrection. We face our own death in the confidence of our faith, knowing that death is defeated. On the other side of death, our Lord Jesus has for us eternal life and salvation.

On His way to raise Lazarus, who had been dead for four days, Jesus is met by Martha. In the midst of her tears, Jesus teaches her about life, death, and the resurrection. The words of comfort that Jesus spoke to Martha are also for us and our comfort: "Jesus said to her, 'I am the resurrection and the life. Whoever believes in Me, though he die, yet shall he live, and everyone who lives and believes in Me shall never die' " (John 11:25–26).

Because of Jesus and His death, because He took all the punishment for our sin, because all of our sins are forgiven, and because we are His people, marked with His name in our Baptism, we have nothing to fear in death. Faith knows that Jesus brings us death as a gift. This is a mystery: just as Jesus destroyed death by dying, so He gives His Christians life through their death. Though we die, yet we shall live. For the Christian, death is the final answer to our daily petition in the Lord's Prayer, "Deliver us from evil." When we die, we will pray that prayer no more; it will be answered. Our death is a gift from Jesus to bring us from death to life.

GRIEF:
WHAT TO EXPECT

But we do not want you to be uninformed, brothers, about those who are asleep, that you may not grieve as others do who have no hope.

—1 Thessalonians 4:13

When we say, "I hope it rains," we indicate that we do not know if it will, and even though we assume it will not, we would like it to rain. There is an embedded uncertainty when we use the word *hope*.

The opposite is true in the Scriptures. In the Bible, hope is not something uncertain or unsure. Because what we hope will come to pass is promised by God, and because God never lies, our hope is sure and certain. Hope, in the Bible, is faith directed toward the future. So when we speak of the *hope of the resurrection*, we are not saying, "I'm not sure if there will be a resurrection, but it would be nice if there were." No. In the Scriptures, hope (like faith) is casting all doubt aside. We are then saying, "God has promised to raise me and all flesh from death, and give to me and all believers in Him eternal life. So I yearn and pray and eagerly expect the resurrection of the body and the life everlasting."

As Christians, we know that there is nothing wrong or sinful about grief. The Gospel sets us free to mourn and be sad at the death of our loved one. But we also rejoice that the Lord Jesus has overcome death, and He is with us in our grief. Death and sorrow cannot overcome Him, and so they cannot overcome us. The verse that speaks most clearly to the mourning Christian is 1 Thessalonians 4:13: "But we do not want you to be uninformed, brothers, about those who are asleep, that you may not grieve as others do who have no hope." We grieve, we mourn, but this is not without hope. We cry and laugh; we weep and smile; we are sad and we trust in the Lord.

Psalm 23:4 offers a wonderful road map as we travel the road of grief:

> Even though I walk through the valley
> of the shadow of death, I will fear no
> evil, for You are with me; Your rod and
> Your staff, they comfort me.

We take comfort in the assurance that the Lord is with us. We do not grieve alone. And we take comfort in the knowledge that though the way seems dark and death seems very close, Jesus is on the path with us to care for us. There is no place for fear with the Lord at our side. Finally, we know that we are passing through the valley. We are not here to stay. The darkness of grief will give way to the joy of Jesus' gift of forgiveness and life.

Grief brings with it different waves of emotions. Each person grieves differently, but there are some emotions that we might expect, and the hope we have in our Good Shepherd, Jesus, offers us comfort in the midst of these struggles.

Expect Shock . . .
and Acceptance

The news of a loved one's death is jarring, disorienting. "How can this be? This can't be true." In a moment, everything changes. The truth is sometimes too difficult to accept. It takes time for the reality of death to settle in.

The funeral service is an important part of this process of acceptance. In the funeral, the reality of death is matched with the reality of Jesus' death. No matter how much we are tossed around by our emotions, the love of Jesus is always secure.

It is often helpful for those who are mourning to tell the story of the death of loved ones. This helps grasp what has happened and place this death in the context of life. A listening ear is a true gift, and it is a wonderful privilege to be entrusted with these stories.

Expect Sadness . . .
and Joy

Death is sad. Funerals are sad. Empty homes and estate sales and holidays without our loved ones are sad. There is a lingering sorrow that follows death, which we call mourning.

Jesus Himself knows what it is like to be sad. Jesus mourned the death of Lazarus. The shortest verse in the Bible concerns this very thing: "Jesus wept" (John 11:35). Jesus cried because He was sad.

The fact that Jesus, the Son of God Himself, knows the deep sadness that death causes gives us peace in the midst of tears. "If Jesus cries, it must be okay for me to cry also." Yes, cry. Death is sad. At the same time we rejoice because the Lord's Word comforts us in sadness: Jesus has overcome death and come out of the grave. He died for us and promises us His love and eternal life.

The devil would use our sadness to push us into a debilitating darkness, a deep sadness that threatens to choke out our faith and love. This is mourning without hope. Sometimes this deep sadness can lead to a physical sickness that needs doctors and medication to address. Other times it is a spiritual condition that needs a constant diet of the Lord's Gospel. Many times it is a combination of these two. Family and your pastor are advisors to gauge if your sadness is dangerous to your health.

Expect Anger, Frustration . . .

and Trust

Death often causes us to question God, especially when death is sudden or tragic. "Why, God? Why her? Why now?" We even question God's love for us: "If you loved him, surely You wouldn't have let that happen. How can You love me and still let me hurt so much?" In the agony of death and the pain of suffering, God seems far away, like He's angry or does not care.

We do not know why the Lord gives out death the way He does. We do not know why this person suffers so much while that person does not. The Lord has not told us. The danger here is this: we try and figure out how the Lord feels about us based on the circumstances of our life. "If things are going well, then God must love me." Then the opposite would be true: "If things are rotten, God must hate me." But the Lord has not given us the circumstances of our life as the thermometer of His love. For this He has given the cross.

There is absolute certainty for the grieving that God loves them: Jesus died. This is the final verdict of the Lord's feelings for us, of His love.

For I am sure that neither death nor life, nor angels nor rulers, nor things present nor things to come, nor powers, nor height nor depth, nor anything else in all creation, will be able to separate us from the love of God in Christ Jesus our Lord. (Romans 8:38–39)

We might not know why God has given out this or that suffering, but we trust that He loves us, died for us, and has us as His own dear children.

Expect Regret . . .
and Forgiveness

After the death of a loved one, our consciences are often troubled with regret. There are things we wish we would have done and said, and things we wish we would not have done or said. Often we sinned against our loved ones—that is what sinners do.

We are prone to make excuses and attempt to ease the pain of our guilt, but this cannot undo what has been done. Beware of excusing sin. The Gospel never excuses sin. The Gospel forgives sin. The sins that we commit against our family and friends are sins for which Jesus died. His blood covers them all. We are forgiven.

Expect Loneliness . . .
and Comfort

Death brings feelings of emptiness. The days and weeks following the death of a loved one are hectic, but eventually relatives return to their homes, friends go back to their routines, and mourners are left alone. Holidays, anniversaries, and birthdays are also times of loneliness.

The Lord has comfort for the lonely. He has promised His abiding presence: "You are with me" (Psalm 23:4). "I will never leave you nor forsake you" (Hebrews 13:5). "And behold, I am with you always, to the end of the age" (Matthew 28:20).

The Lord also gives us fellow Christians. The fellowship of the Church is a wonderful consolation to the lonely. The Holy Spirit gathers us to His Word and Sacraments with other believers. These are able to offer friendship and love, as we "bear one another's burdens" (Galatians 6:2).

Finally, we have the promise that we will see our loved ones again (see 1 Thessalonians 4:15–16).

They are with Jesus now; we will be with Him soon.

The best is yet to come. The Scriptures always hold before us the sure and certain hope of the resurrection of the body and the life everlasting. On the Last Day, the Lord will bring an end to death and wipe away all our tears (see Revelation 7:17; 21:4; Isaiah 25:8; 30:19; 35:10). There is a time coming soon when mourning and crying will cease, when death itself will come to an end, when joy will have no interruption. Our tear-filled eyes stay fixed on the cross of our Lord and our hearts yearn for that great day. "Come, Lord Jesus."

Selected Hymns

Abide with Me

Abide with me, fast falls the eventide.
The darkness deepens; Lord, with me abide.
When other helpers fail and comforts flee,
Help of the helpless, O abide with me.

I need Thy presence ev'ry passing hour;
What but Thy grace can foil the tempter's pow'r?
Who like Thyself my guide and stay can be?
Through cloud and sunshine, O abide with me.

Come not in terrors, as the King of kings,
But kind and good, with healing in Thy wings;
Tears for all woes, a heart for ev'ry plea.
Come, Friend of sinners, thus abide with me.

Swift to its close ebbs out life's little day;
Earth's joys grow dim, its glories pass away;
Change and decay in all around I see;
O Thou who changest not, abide with me.

I fear no foe with Thee at hand to bless;
Ills have no weight and tears no bitterness.
Where is death's sting? Where, grave, thy victory?
I triumph still if Thou abide with me!

Hold Thou Thy cross before my closing eyes;
Shine through the gloom, and point me to the skies.
Heav'n's morning breaks, and earth's vain shadows
    flee;
In life, in death, O Lord, abide with me. (*LSB* 878)

Come unto Me, Ye Weary

"Come unto Me, ye weary,
> And I will give you rest."
O blessèd voice of Jesus,
> Which comes to hearts oppressed!
It tells of benediction,
> Of pardon, grace, and peace,
Of joy that hath no ending,
> Of love that cannot cease.

"Come unto Me, ye fainting,
> And I will give you life."
O cheering voice of Jesus,
> Which comes to aid our strife!
The foe is stern and eager,
> The fight is fierce and long;
But Thou hast made us mighty
> And stronger than the strong.

"And whosoever cometh,
> I will not cast him out."
O patient love of Jesus,
> Which drives away our doubt,
Which, though we be unworthy
> Of love so great and free,
Invites us very sinners
> To come, dear Lord, to Thee! (*LSB* 684:1, 3, 4)

For All the Saints

For all the saints who from their labors rest,
Who Thee by faith before the world confessed,
Thy name, O Jesus, be forever blest.
    Alleluia! Alleluia!

Thou wast their rock, their fortress, and their might;
Thou, Lord, their captain in the well-fought fight;
Thou, in the darkness drear, their one true light.
    Alleluia! Alleluia!

Oh, may Thy soldiers, faithful, true, and bold,
Fight as the saints who nobly fought of old
And win with them the victor's crown of gold!
    Alleluia! Alleluia!

Oh, blest communion, fellowship divine!
We feebly struggle, they in glory shine;
Yet all are one in Thee, for all are Thine.
    Alleluia! Alleluia!

And when the fight is fierce, the warfare long,
Steals on the ear the distant triumph song,
And hearts are brave again, and arms are strong.
    Alleluia! Alleluia!

The golden evening brightens in the west;
Soon, soon to faithful warriors cometh rest;
Sweet is the calm of paradise the blest.
    Alleluia! Alleluia!

But, lo, there breaks a yet more glorious day:
The saints triumphant rise in bright array;
The King of Glory passes on His way.
    Alleluia! Alleluia!

From earth's wide bounds, from ocean's farthest
    coast,
Through gates of pearl streams in the countless
    host,
Singing to Father, Son, and Holy Ghost:
    Alleluia! Alleluia! (*LSB* 677)

Have No Fear, Little Flock

Have no fear, little flock;
Have no fear, little flock,
    For the Father has chosen
    To give you the Kingdom;
Have no fear, little flock!

Have good cheer, little flock;
Have good cheer, little flock,
    For the Father will keep you
    In His love forever;
Have good cheer, little flock!

Praise the Lord high above;
Praise the Lord high above,
    For He stoops down to heal you,
    Uplift and restore you;
Praise the Lord high above!

Thankful hearts raise to God;
Thankful hearts raise to God,
    For He stays close beside you,
    In all things works with you;
Thankful hearts raise to God! (*LSB* 735)

I Know That My Redeemer Lives

I know that my Redeemer lives;
What comfort this sweet sentence gives!
He lives, He lives, who once was dead;
He lives, my ever-living head.

He lives triumphant from the grave;
He lives eternally to save;
He lives all-glorious in the sky;
He lives exalted there on high.

He lives to bless me with His love;
He lives to plead for me above;
He lives my hungry soul to feed;
He lives to help in time of need.

He lives to grant me rich supply;
He lives to guide me with His eye;
He lives to comfort me when faint;
He lives to hear my soul's complaint.

He lives to silence all my fears;
He lives to wipe away my tears;
He lives to calm my troubled heart;
He lives all blessings to impart.

He lives, my kind, wise, heav'nly friend;
He lives and loves me to the end;
He lives, and while He lives, I'll sing;
He lives, my Prophet, Priest, and King.

He lives and grants me daily breath;
He lives, and I shall conquer death;
He lives my mansion to prepare;
He lives to bring me safely there.

He lives, all glory to His name!
He lives, my Jesus, still the same;
Oh, the sweet joy this sentence gives:
I know that my Redeemer lives! (*LSB* 461)

Jesus Lives! The Victory's Won

Jesus lives! The vict'ry's won!
    Death no longer can appall me;
Jesus lives! Death's reign is done!
    From the grave will Christ recall me.
Brighter scenes will then commence;
This shall be my confidence.

Jesus lives! To Him the throne
High above all things is given.
I shall go where He is gone,
Live and reign with Him in heaven.
God is faithful; doubtings, hence!
This shall be my confidence.

Jesus lives! For me He died,
Hence will I, to Jesus living,
Pure in heart and act abide,
Praise to Him and glory giving.
All I need God will dispense;
This shall be my confidence.

Jesus lives! I know full well
Nothing me from Him shall sever.
Neither death nor pow'rs of hell
Part me now from Christ forever.
God will be my sure defense;
This shall be my confidence.

Jesus lives! And now is death
But the gate of life immortal;
This shall calm my trembling breath
When I pass its gloomy portal.
Faith shall cry, as fails each sense:
Jesus is my confidence! (*LSB* 490)

Oh, How Blest Are They

Oh, how blest are they whose toils are ended,
Who through death have unto God ascended!
They have arisen
From the cares which keep us still in prison.

We are still as in a dungeon living,
Still oppressed with sorrow and misgiving;
Our undertakings
Are but toils and troubles and heartbreakings.

They meanwhile are in their chambers sleeping,
Quiet and set free from all their weeping;
No cross or sadness
There can hinder their untroubled gladness.

Christ has wiped away their tears forever;
They have that for which we still endeavor.
By them are chanted
Songs that ne'er to mortal ears were granted.

Come, O Christ, and loose the chains that bind us;
Lead us forth and cast this world behind us.
With You, the Anointed,
Finds the soul its joy and rest appointed. (*LSB* 679)

Oh, What Their Joy

Oh, what their joy and their glory must be,
Those endless Sabbaths the blessèd ones see!
> Crowns for the valiant, to weary ones rest;
> God shall be all, and in all ever blest.

In new Jerusalem joy shall be found,
Blessings of peace shall forever abound;
> Wish and fulfillment are not severed there,
> Nor the things prayed for come short of the
> prayer.

We, where no trouble distraction can bring,
Safely the anthems of Zion shall sing;
> While for Your grace, Lord, their voices of
> praise
> Your blessèd people shall evermore raise.

Now let us worship our Lord and our King,
Joyfully raising our voices to sing:
> Praise to the Father, and praise to the Son,
> Praise to the Spirit, to God, Three in One.
> (*LSB* 675)

This Body in the Grave We Lay

This body in the grave we lay
There to await that solemn day
When God Himself shall bid it rise
To mount triumphant to the skies.

And so to earth we now entrust
What came from dust and turns to dust
And from the dust shall rise that day
In glorious triumph o'er decay.

The soul forever lives with God,
Who freely hath His grace bestowed
And through His Son redeemed it here
From ev'ry sin, from ev'ry fear.

All trials and all griefs are past,
A blessèd end has come at last.
Christ's yoke was borne with ready will;
Who dieth thus is living still.

We have no cause to mourn or weep;
Securely shall this body sleep
Till Christ Himself shall death destroy
And raise the blessèd dead to joy.

Then let us leave this place of rest
And homeward turn, for they are blest

Who heed God's warning and prepare
Lest death should find them unaware.

So help us, Jesus, ground of faith;
Thou hast redeemed us by Thy death
From endless death and set us free.
We laud and praise and worship Thee. (*LSB* 759)

Through Jesus' Blood and Merit

Through Jesus' blood and merit
    I am at peace with God.
What, then, can daunt my spirit,
    However dark my road?
My courage shall not fail me,
    For God is on my side;
Though hell itself assail me,
    Its rage I may deride.

There's nothing that can sever
    From this great love of God;
No want, no pain whatever,
    No famine, peril, flood.

Though thousand foes surround me,
 For slaughter mark His sheep,
They never shall confound me,
 The vict'ry I shall reap.

For neither life's temptation
 Nor death's most trying hour
Nor angels of high station
 Nor any other pow'r
Nor things that now are present
 Nor things that are to come
Nor height, however pleasant,
 Nor darkest depths of gloom

Nor any creature ever
 Shall from the love of God
This ransomed sinner sever;
 For in my Savior's blood
This love has its foundation;
 God hears my faithful prayer
And long before creation
 Named me His child and heir. (*LSB* 746)

SELECTED
PSALMS

Answer Me When I Call

Psalm 4

1 Answer me when I call, O God of my righteousness!
> You have given me relief when I was in distress.
> Be gracious to me and hear my prayer!

2 O men, how long shall my honor be turned into shame?
> How long will you love vain words and seek after
> lies?

3 But know that the LORD has set apart the godly for
Himself;
> the LORD hears when I call to Him.

4 Be angry, and do not sin;
> ponder in your own hearts on your beds, and be
> silent.

5 Offer right sacrifices,
> and put your trust in the LORD.

6 There are many who say, "Who will show us some good?
> Lift up the light of Your face upon us, O LORD!"

7 You have put more joy in my heart
> than they have when their grain and wine abound.

8 In peace I will both lie down and sleep;
> for You alone, O LORD, make me dwell in safety.

Lead Me in Your Righteousness
Psalm 5

¹ Give ear to my words, O Lord;
　　consider my groaning.
² Give attention to the sound of my cry,
　　my King and my God,
　　for to You do I pray.
³ O Lord, in the morning You hear my voice;
　　in the morning I prepare a sacrifice for You
　　　and watch.
⁴ For You are not a God who delights in wickedness;
　　evil may not dwell with You.
⁵ The boastful shall not stand before Your eyes;
　　You hate all evildoers.
⁶ You destroy those who speak lies;
　　the Lord abhors the bloodthirsty and
　　　deceitful man.
⁷ But I, through the abundance of Your steadfast love,
　　will enter Your house.
I will bow down toward Your holy temple
　　in the fear of You.
⁸ Lead me, O Lord, in Your righteousness because of
　my enemies;
　　make Your way straight before me.
⁹ For there is no truth in their mouth;
　　their inmost self is destruction;
their throat is an open grave;
　　they flatter with their tongue.

¹⁰ Make them bear their guilt, O God;
>   let them fall by their own counsels;
because of the abundance of their transgressions cast
>   them out,
>   for they have rebelled against You.
¹¹ But let all who take refuge in You rejoice;
>   let them ever sing for joy,
and spread Your protection over them,
>   that those who love Your name may exult in You.
¹² For You bless the righteous, O Lord;
>   You cover him with favor as with a shield.

O Lord, Deliver My Life

Psalm 6

¹ O Lord, rebuke me not in Your anger,
>   nor discipline me in Your wrath.
² Be gracious to me, O Lord, for I am languishing;
>   heal me, O Lord, for my bones are troubled.
³ My soul also is greatly troubled.
>   But You, O Lord—how long?
⁴ Turn, O Lord, deliver my life;
>   save me for the sake of Your steadfast love.
⁵ For in death there is no remembrance of You;
>   in Sheol who will give You praise?
⁶ I am weary with my moaning;

every night I flood my bed with tears;
 I drench my couch with my weeping.
[7] My eye wastes away because of grief;
 it grows weak because of all my foes.
[8] Depart from me, all you workers of evil,
 for the LORD has heard the sound of my weeping.
[9] The LORD has heard my plea;
 the LORD accepts my prayer.
[10] All my enemies shall be ashamed and greatly troubled;
 they shall turn back and be put to shame in a moment.

Peace and Hope

Psalm 16

[1] Preserve me, O God, for in You I take refuge.
[2] I say to the LORD, "You are my Lord;
 I have no good apart from You."
[3] As for the saints in the land, they are the excellent ones,
 in whom is all my delight.
[4] The sorrows of those who run after another god shall multiply;
 their drink offerings of blood I will not pour out
 or take their names on my lips.
[5] The LORD is my chosen portion and my cup;
 You hold my lot.
[6] The lines have fallen for me in pleasant places;
 indeed, I have a beautiful inheritance.

⁷ I bless the LORD who gives me counsel;
in the night also my heart instructs me.
⁸ I have set the LORD always before me;
because He is at my right hand, I shall not be shaken.
⁹ Therefore my heart is glad, and my whole being rejoices;
my flesh also dwells secure.
¹⁰ For You will not abandon my soul to Sheol,
or let Your holy one see corruption.
¹¹ You make known to me the path of life;
in Your presence there is fullness of joy;
at Your right hand are pleasures forevermore.

The Lord Is My Shepherd
Psalm 23

¹ The LORD is my shepherd; I shall not want.
² He makes me lie down in green pastures.
He leads me beside still waters.
³ He restores my soul.
He leads me in paths of righteousness
for His name's sake.
⁴ Even though I walk through the valley of the shadow of
death,
I will fear no evil,
for You are with me;
Your rod and Your staff,
they comfort me.
⁵ You prepare a table before me
in the presence of my enemies;

You anoint my head with oil;
    my cup overflows.
6 Surely goodness and mercy shall follow me
    all the days of my life,
and I shall dwell in the house of the Lord
    forever.

Forgiveness and Redemption
Psalm 32:1–5

1 Blessed is the one whose transgression is forgiven,
    whose sin is covered.
2 Blessed is the man against whom the Lord counts no
iniquity,
    and in whose spirit there is no deceit.
3 For when I kept silent, my bones wasted away
    through my groaning all day long.
4 For day and night Your hand was heavy upon me;
    my strength was dried up as by the heat of summer.
    Selah
5 I acknowledged my sin to You,
    and I did not cover my iniquity;
I said, "I will confess my transgressions to the Lord,"
    and You forgave the iniquity of my sin. *Selah*

Consolation and Comfort
Psalm 38:9, 21–22

⁹ O Lord, all my longing is before You;
    my sighing is not hidden from You.
²¹ Do not forsake me, O Lᴏʀᴅ!
    O my God, be not far from me!
²² Make haste to help me,
    O Lord, my salvation!

Have Mercy on Me
Psalm 51

¹ Have mercy on me, O God,
    according to Your steadfast love;
according to Your abundant mercy
    blot out my transgressions.
² Wash me thoroughly from my iniquity,
    and cleanse me from my sin!
³ For I know my transgressions,
    and my sin is ever before me.
⁴ Against You, You only, have I sinned
    and done what is evil in Your sight,
so that You may be justified in Your words
    and blameless in Your judgment.
⁵ Behold, I was brought forth in iniquity,
    and in sin did my mother conceive me.

⁶ Behold, You delight in truth in the inward being,
  and You teach me wisdom in the secret heart.
⁷ Purge me with hyssop, and I shall be clean;
  wash me, and I shall be whiter than snow.
⁸ Let me hear joy and gladness;
  let the bones that You have broken rejoice.
⁹ Hide Your face from my sins,
  and blot out all my iniquities.
¹⁰ Create in me a clean heart, O God,
  and renew a right spirit within me.
¹¹ Cast me not away from Your presence,
  and take not Your Holy Spirit from me.
¹² Restore to me the joy of Your salvation,
  and uphold me with a willing spirit.
¹³ Then I will teach transgressors Your ways,
  and sinners will return to You.
¹⁴ Deliver me from bloodguiltiness, O God,
  O God of my salvation,
  and my tongue will sing aloud of Your
  righteousness.
¹⁵ O Lord, open my lips,
  and my mouth will declare Your praise.
¹⁶ For You will not delight in sacrifice, or I would give it;
  You will not be pleased with a burnt offering.
¹⁷ The sacrifices of God are a broken spirit;
  a broken and contrite heart, O God, You will not
  despise.
¹⁸ Do good to Zion in Your good pleasure;
  build up the walls of Jerusalem;
¹⁹ then will You delight in right sacrifices,
  in burnt offerings and whole burnt offerings;
  then bulls will be offered on Your altar.

Hope

Psalm 90

¹ Lord, You have been our dwelling place
    in all generations.
² Before the mountains were brought forth,
    or ever You had formed the earth and the world,
    from everlasting to everlasting You are God.
³ You return man to dust
    and say, "Return, O children of man!"
⁴ For a thousand years in Your sight
    are but as yesterday when it is past,
    or as a watch in the night.
⁵ You sweep them away as with a flood; they are like
a dream,
    like grass that is renewed in the morning:
⁶ in the morning it flourishes and is renewed;
    in the evening it fades and withers.
⁷ For we are brought to an end by Your anger;
    by Your wrath we are dismayed.
⁸ You have set our iniquities before You,
    our secret sins in the light of Your presence.
⁹ For all our days pass away under Your wrath;
    we bring our years to an end like a sigh.
¹⁰ The years of our life are seventy,
    or even by reason of strength eighty;
yet their span is but toil and trouble;
    they are soon gone, and we fly away.
¹¹ Who considers the power of Your anger,
    and Your wrath according to the fear of You?

¹² So teach us to number our days
　　　　that we may get a heart of wisdom.
¹³ Return, O Lᴏʀᴅ! How long?
　　　　Have pity on Your servants!
¹⁴ Satisfy us in the morning with Your steadfast love,
　　　　that we may rejoice and be glad all our days.
¹⁵ Make us glad for as many days as You have afflicted us,
　　　　and for as many years as we have seen evil.
¹⁶ Let Your work be shown to Your servants,
　　　　and Your glorious power to their children.
¹⁷ Let the favor of the Lord our God be upon us,
　　　　and establish the work of our hands upon us;
　　　　yes, establish the work of our hands!

Sing to the Lord
Psalm 98

¹ Oh sing to the Lᴏʀᴅ a new song,
　　　　for He has done marvelous things!
His right hand and His holy arm
　　　　have worked salvation for Him.
² The Lᴏʀᴅ has made known His salvation;
　　　　He has revealed His righteousness in the sight of
　　　　the nations.
³ He has remembered His steadfast love and faithfulness
　　　　to the house of Israel.
All the ends of the earth have seen
　　　　the salvation of our God.

⁴ Make a joyful noise to the Lᴏʀᴅ, all the earth;
  break forth into joyous song and sing praises!
⁵ Sing praises to the Lᴏʀᴅ with the lyre,
  with the lyre and the sound of melody!
⁶ With trumpets and the sound of the horn
  make a joyful noise before the King, the Lᴏʀᴅ!
⁷ Let the sea roar, and all that fills it;
  the world and those who dwell in it!
⁸ Let the rivers clap their hands;
  let the hills sing for joy together
⁹ before the Lᴏʀᴅ, for He comes
  to judge the earth.
He will judge the world with righteousness,
  and the peoples with equity.

Consolation and Comfort
Psalm 102:1–2

¹ Hear my prayer, O Lᴏʀᴅ;
let my cry come to You!
² Do not hide Your face from me
  in the day of my distress!
Incline Your ear to me;
  answer me speedily in the day when I call!

Assurance

Psalm 119:9–17

⁹ How can a young man keep his way pure?
    By guarding it according to Your word.
¹⁰ With my whole heart I seek You;
    let me not wander from Your commandments!
¹¹ I have stored up Your word in my heart,
    that I might not sin against You.
¹² Blessed are You, O Lord;
    teach me Your statutes!
¹³ With my lips I declare
    all the rules of Your mouth.
¹⁴ In the way of Your testimonies I delight
    as much as in all riches.
¹⁵ I will meditate on Your precepts
    and fix my eyes on Your ways.
¹⁶ I will delight in Your statutes;
    I will not forget Your word.
¹⁷ Deal bountifully with Your servant,
    that I may live and keep Your word.

Your Promise Gives Me Life

Psalm 119:49–56

⁴⁹ Remember Your word to Your servant,
    in which You have made me hope.

⁵⁰ This is my comfort in my affliction,
that Your promise gives me life.
⁵¹ The insolent utterly deride me,
but I do not turn away from Your law.
⁵² When I think of Your rules from of old,
I take comfort, O Lord.
⁵³ Hot indignation seizes me because of the wicked,
who forsake Your law.
⁵⁴ Your statutes have been my songs
in the house of my sojourning.
⁵⁵ I remember Your name in the night, O Lord,
and keep Your law.
⁵⁶ This blessing has fallen to me,
that I have kept Your precepts.

I Cry to You

Psalm 130:1–5

¹ Out of the depths I cry to You, O Lord!
² O Lord, hear my voice!
Let Your ears be attentive
to the voice of my pleas for mercy!
³ If You, O Lord, should mark iniquities,
O Lord, who could stand?
⁴ But with You there is forgiveness,
that You may be feared.
⁵ I wait for the Lord, my soul waits,
and in His word I hope.

Lord, You Know Me

Psalm 139:1–12, 23–24

¹ O Lord, You have searched me and known me!
² You know when I sit down and when I rise up;
    You discern my thoughts from afar.
³ You search out my path and my lying down
    and are acquainted with all my ways.
⁴ Even before a word is on my tongue,
    behold, O Lord, You know it altogether.
⁵ You hem me in, behind and before,
    and lay Your hand upon me.
⁶ Such knowledge is too wonderful for me;
    it is high; I cannot attain it.
⁷ Where shall I go from Your Spirit?
    Or where shall I flee from Your presence?
⁸ If I ascend to heaven, You are there!
    If I make my bed in Sheol, You are there!
⁹ If I take the wings of the morning
    and dwell in the uttermost parts of the sea,
¹⁰ even there Your hand shall lead me,
    and Your right hand shall hold me.
¹¹ If I say, "Surely the darkness shall cover me,
    and the light about me be night,"
¹² even the darkness is not dark to You;
    the night is bright as the day,
    for darkness is as light with You.

²³ Search me, O God, and know my heart!
    Try me and know my thoughts!
²⁴ And see if there be any grievous way in me,
    and lead me in the way everlasting!

SELECTED SCRIPTURE PASSAGES

The Dead Will Return   Isaiah 25:7–8; 35:10

^{25:7}[The Lord] will swallow up on this mountain
    the covering that is cast over all peoples,
    the veil that is spread over all nations.
  ⁸He will swallow up death forever;
and the Lord God will wipe away tears from all faces,
    and the reproach of His people He will take away
      from all the earth,
    for the Lord has spoken.

^{35:10}And the ransomed of the Lord shall return
    and come to Zion with singing;
everlasting joy shall be upon their heads;
    they shall obtain gladness and joy,
      and sorrow and sighing shall flee away.

Waiting for the Lord   Lamentations 3:22–26

²²The steadfast love of the Lord never ceases;
    His mercies never come to an end;
²³they are new every morning;
    great is Your faithfulness.
²⁴"The Lord is my portion," says my soul,
    "therefore I will hope in Him."
²⁵The Lord is good to those who wait for Him,
    to the soul who seeks Him.
²⁶It is good that one should wait quietly
    for the salvation of the Lord.

Return to the Lord Hosea 6:1

¹"Come, let us return to the Lord;
  for He has torn us, that He may heal us;
    He has struck us down, and He will bind us up."

Saved through God's Son John 3:17

¹⁷For God did not send His Son into the world to condemn the world, but in order that the world might be saved through Him.

A Place Prepared for Us John 14:1–6

¹"Let not your hearts be troubled. Believe in God; believe also in Me. ²In My Father's house are many rooms. If it were not so, would I have told you that I go to prepare a place for you? ³And if I go and prepare a place for you, I will come again and will take you to Myself, that where I am you may be also. ⁴And you know the way to where I am going." ⁵Thomas said to Him, "Lord, we do not know where You are going. How can we know the way?" ⁶Jesus said to him, "I am the way, and the truth, and the life. No one comes to the Father except through Me."

Saved by God's Love Romans 5:8–9

⁸God shows His love for us in that while we were still sinners, Christ died for us. ⁹Since, therefore, we have now been justified by His blood, much more shall we be saved by Him from the wrath of God.

Baptized into Christ's Death Romans 6:3–9

³Do you not know that all of us who have been baptized into Christ Jesus were baptized into His death? ⁴We were buried therefore with Him by baptism into death, in order that, just as Christ was raised from the dead by the glory of the Father, we too might walk in newness of life.

⁵For if we have been united with Him in a death like His, we shall certainly be united with Him in a resurrection like His. ⁶We know that our old self was crucified with Him in order that the body of sin might be brought to nothing, so that we would no longer be enslaved to sin. ⁷For one who has died has been set free from sin. ⁸Now if we have died with Christ, we believe that we will also live with Him. ⁹We know that Christ, being raised from the dead, will never die again; death no longer has dominion over Him.

³¹What then shall we say to these things? If God is for us, who can be against us? ³²He who did not spare His own Son but gave Him up for us all, how will He not also with Him graciously give us all things? ³³Who shall bring any charge against God's elect? It is God who justifies. ³⁴Who is to condemn? Christ Jesus is the one who died—more than that, who was raised—who is at the right hand of God, who indeed is interceding for us. ³⁵Who shall separate us from the love of Christ? Shall tribulation, or distress, or persecution, or famine, or nakedness, or danger, or sword? ³⁶As it is written,

"For Your sake we are being killed all the day long;
　　we are regarded as sheep to be slaughtered."

³⁷No, in all these things we are more than conquerors through Him who loved us.

Mystery of the Resurrection

I Corinthians 15:51–58

⁵¹Behold! I tell you a mystery. We shall not all sleep, but we shall all be changed, ⁵²in a moment, in the twinkling of an eye, at the last trumpet. For the trumpet will sound, and the dead will be raised imperishable, and we shall be changed. ⁵³For this perishable body must put on the imperishable, and this mortal body must put on immortality.

⁵⁴When the perishable puts on the imperishable, and the mortal puts on immortality, then shall come to pass the saying that is written:

> "Death is swallowed up in victory."
> ⁵⁵"O death, where is your victory?
>   O death, where is your sting?"

⁵⁶The sting of death is sin, and the power of sin is the law. ⁵⁷But thanks be to God, who gives us the victory through our Lord Jesus Christ.

⁵⁸Therefore, my beloved brothers, be steadfast, immovable, always abounding in the work of the Lord, knowing that in the Lord your labor is not in vain.

The Perishable Raised Imperishable

I Corinthians 15:42–49

⁴²So is it with the resurrection of the dead. What is sown is perishable; what is raised is imperishable. ⁴³It is sown in dishonor; it is raised in glory. It is sown in weakness; it is raised in power. ⁴⁴It is sown a natural body; it is raised a spiritual body. If there is a natural body, there is also a spiritual body. ⁴⁵Thus it is written, "The first man Adam became a living being"; the last Adam became a life-giving spirit. ⁴⁶But it is not the spiritual that is first but the natural, and then the spiritual. ⁴⁷The first man was from the earth, a man of dust; the second man is from heaven. ⁴⁸As

was the man of dust, so also are those who are of the dust, and as is the man of heaven, so also are those who are of heaven. ⁴⁹Just as we have borne the image of the man of dust, we shall also bear the image of the man of heaven.

God of All Comfort 2 Corinthians 1:3–7

³Blessed be the God and Father of our Lord Jesus Christ, the Father of mercies and God of all comfort, ⁴who comforts us in all our affliction, so that we may be able to comfort those who are in any affliction, with the comfort with which we ourselves are comforted by God. ⁵For as we share abundantly in Christ's sufferings, so through Christ we share abundantly in comfort too. ⁶If we are afflicted, it is for your comfort and salvation; and if we are comforted, it is for your comfort, which you experience when you patiently endure the same sufferings that we suffer. ⁷Our hope for you is unshaken, for we know that as you share in our sufferings, you will also share in our comfort.

Eternal Hope 1 Thessalonians 4:13–18

¹³But we do not want you to be uninformed, brothers, about those who are asleep, that you may not grieve as others do who have no hope. ¹⁴For since we believe that Jesus died and rose again, even so, through Jesus, God will bring with Him those who have fallen asleep. ¹⁵For this

we declare to you by a word from the Lord, that we who are alive, who are left until the coming of the Lord, will not precede those who have fallen asleep. ¹⁶For the Lord Himself will descend from heaven with a cry of command, with the voice of an archangel, and with the sound of the trumpet of God. And the dead in Christ will rise first. ¹⁷Then we who are alive, who are left, will be caught up together with them in the clouds to meet the Lord in the air, and so we will always be with the Lord. ¹⁸Therefore encourage one another with these words.

A God Who Sympathizes with Us

Hebrews 4:9–10; 14–16

⁹So then, there remains a Sabbath rest for the people of God, ¹⁰for whoever has entered God's rest has also rested from his works as God did from His.

¹⁴Since then we have a great high priest who has passed through the heavens, Jesus, the Son of God, let us hold fast our confession. ¹⁵For we do not have a high priest who is unable to sympathize with our weaknesses, but one who in every respect has been tempted as we are, yet without sin. ¹⁶Let us then with confidence draw near to the throne of grace, that we may receive mercy and find grace to help in time of need.

Don't Grow Weary Hebrews 12:1–4

¹Therefore, since we are surrounded by so great a cloud of witnesses, let us also lay aside every weight, and sin which clings so closely, and let us run with endurance the race that is set before us, ²looking to Jesus, the founder and perfecter of our faith, who for the joy that was set before Him endured the cross, despising the shame, and is seated at the right hand of the throne of God.

³Consider Him who endured from sinners such hostility against Himself, so that you may not grow weary or fainthearted. ⁴In your struggle against sin you have not yet resisted to the point of shedding your blood.

Redeemed in the Blood of the Lamb

Revelation 7:9–17

⁹After this I looked, and behold, a great multitude that no one could number, from every nation, from all tribes and peoples and languages, standing before the throne and before the Lamb, clothed in white robes, with palm branches in their hands, ¹⁰and crying out with a loud voice, "Salvation belongs to our God who sits on the throne, and to the Lamb!" ¹¹And all the angels were standing around the throne and around the elders and the four living creatures, and they fell on their faces before the throne and worshiped God, ¹²saying, "Amen! Blessing and glory and wisdom and thanksgiving and honor and power and might be to our

God forever and ever! Amen."

¹³Then one of the elders addressed me, saying, "Who are these, clothed in white robes, and from where have they come?" ¹⁴I said to him, "Sir, you know." And he said to me, "These are the ones coming out of the great tribulation. They have washed their robes and made them white in the blood of the Lamb.

¹⁵"Therefore they are before the throne of God,
    and serve Him day and night in His temple;
    and He who sits on the throne will shelter them
      with His presence.
¹⁶They shall hunger no more, neither thirst anymore;
    the sun shall not strike them,
    nor any scorching heat.
¹⁷For the Lamb in the midst of the throne will be their
  shepherd,
    and He will guide them to springs of living water,
and God will wipe away every tear from their eyes."

The New Heaven and the New Earth

Revelation 21:1–7

¹Then I saw a new heaven and a new earth, for the first heaven and the first earth had passed away, and the sea was no more. ²And I saw the holy city, new Jerusalem, coming down out of heaven from God, prepared as a bride adorned for her husband. ³And I heard a loud voice from the throne saying, "Behold, the dwelling place of God is with man. He

will dwell with them, and they will be His people, and God Himself will be with them as their God. [4]He will wipe away every tear from their eyes, and death shall be no more, neither shall there be mourning, nor crying, nor pain anymore, for the former things have passed away."

[5]And He who was seated on the throne said, "Behold, I am making all things new." Also He said, "Write this down, for these words are trustworthy and true." [6]And He said to me, "It is done! I am the Alpha and the Omega, the beginning and the end. To the thirsty I will give from the spring of the water of life without payment. [7]The one who conquers will have this heritage, and I will be his God and he will be My son."

The Apostles' Creed

I believe in God, the Father Almighty, Maker of heaven and earth.

And in Jesus Christ, His only Son, our Lord, who was conceived by the Holy Spirit, born of the Virgin Mary, suffered under Pontius Pilate, was crucified, died and was buried. He descended into hell. The third day He rose again from the dead. He ascended into heaven and sits at the right hand of God, the Father Almighty. From thence He will come to judge the living and the dead.

I believe in the Holy Spirit, the holy Christian church, the communion of saints, the forgiveness of sins, the resurrection of the body, and the life everlasting. Amen.

PRAYERS for OURSELVES and OTHERS

After a Loved One's Expected Death

O God, I am filled with deep grief and loss. My loved one and I went through the caregiving journey together, and even though I was expecting this, it's still very difficult to know that he (she) is gone. Comfort me, and give me strength to fill the emptiness in my life. Fill me with Your peace and love. Receive my loved one into Your glorious kingdom so that he (she) may rest in Your love, peace, and joy forever. In Jesus' name. Amen. (1)

After the Death of a Loved One

Amid my tears, O Lord, I praise You that You have received (*name*) to Yourself in glory for all eternity. I thank You that You have brought him (her) to the knowledge of Jesus Christ, our Lord and Savior. Comfort all who mourn with the glorious hope of the resurrection and life eternal. Grant me grace to say with a believing heart, "Thy will be done," and to know that Your will is a good and gracious will, even in the present hour. Comfort me through Your Gospel, which promises strength and help to the troubled and weary. O Lord, forsake me not in this hour. Prepare me through Your Word and Sacrament for that day when You will call me to Yourself, that I may joyfully join the whole company of heaven to live with You forever; for Jesus' sake I ask it. Amen. (2)

As I Grieve

As I grieve, O God, help me to express my feelings. Grief is not easy, and sometimes I forget or become confused. I'm told this is normal, but when will my *real* normal return? Help me to get proper rest, eat nutritiously, and exercise. These are things that I was told to do, but I am having trouble doing them now. Comfort me, Lord, with Your love and fill me with the peace that I know only You can give. This I pray in Jesus' name. Amen. (3)

At Christmastime

Heavenly Father, the tree stands in the corner; I got that much done. There are boxes of ornaments to be brought out—so many of them carry memories of (*name*) that I almost cannot bear the thought of decorating the tree. I don't know if I can do this. O God, I don't know if I should do this. The children are expecting presents and music, happiness and joy. And yet the thought of preparing and shopping and singing and a happy family gathering seems to remind me even more of how much I miss (*name*), and it seems wrong to celebrate. It seems like I am not missing him (her) enough if I celebrate the holidays.

Bring me to the remembrance of Your Word, that I may find comfort and peace; bring me to understand that all birth and life stands in the shadow of death, just as Your Son's birth on that first Christmas stood in the shadow of His coming cross. Let me be consoled with the knowledge that You surely work all things for my good, for the good of those who love You and call upon You, even for (*name*) and even for me now. Counsel me in my grief, that I may find Your will for me and become strong again to live and love according to Your will. Above all, assure me once again, in the great story of Christmas, that I am not alone. Emmanuel, God with us. Yes, in Your Son's name I pray. Amen. (4)

At Easter
....

Father in heaven, familiar words have taken new and wondrous meaning since (*name*)'s death. When I confess the Creed and my belief in "the resurrection of the body and the life everlasting," it has become more real to me knowing I will see (*name*) again, in our bodies in the new heaven and earth You will create on that Last Day. When we say to you "Therefore with angels and archangels and the whole company of heaven," I know I am singing "Holy, holy, holy" in unison together with (*name*) in heaven. And when I receive the body and the blood of Your Son, Jesus, in Holy Communion, I am surely participating in a foretaste of the heavenly banquet to come when I will be reunited with (*name*) in Your presence forever.

Now we prepare to greet one another on Easter morning with the familiar words, "He is risen!" "He is risen, indeed. Alleluia!" Even as I choke up with grief and the depth of my missing (*name*), I am once again strengthened by familiar words. The readings of Job's "I know my Redeemer lives!", Paul's strong words that "at the coming of the Lord . . . the dead in Christ will rise," and Jesus' tender greeting to Mary in the garden, heard both at the funeral and again as we celebrate Jesus' resurrection, comfort me. In my sorrow You come to me this Easter and bless me with Your

Word. The Gospel message that You loved me enough to send Your Son to redeem me and (*name*) and all who believe in Jesus from death and the grave—even when we were Your enemies and unlovable because of our sin—strengthens me and assures me of Your love now even in my grief.

Lilies and colored eggs and chocolate and even loved ones will pass away. But with You there is hope and a future. Thank You, Lord, for Your grace and love; in the name of Your resurrected and eternal Son, Jesus. Amen. (5)

Confession and Deliverance

Almighty and merciful God, the Fountain of all goodness, who knows the thoughts of my heart, I confess unto You that I have sinned against You and am evil in Your sight; wash me I implore You from the stains of my past sins, and give me grace and power to put away all hurtful things, so that, being delivered from the bondage of sin, I may bring forth worthy fruits of repentance. O Eternal Light, shine into my heart; O Eternal Goodness, deliver me from evil; O Eternal Power, be to me a support; Eternal Wisdom, scatter the darkness of my ignorance; Eternal Pity, have mercy upon me. Grant to me that with all my heart and mind and strength I may evermore seek Your face, and finally bring me in Your infinite mercy to Your holy presence. So strengthen my weakness that, following in the footsteps of Your blessed Son, I may obtain the promise of my Baptism and enter into Your promised joy; through Jesus Christ, Your Son, my Lord. Amen. (6)

Confident Hope

Lord, I have lost the one whose life was entwined with mine. His (her) love was precious to me. This loss has grieved me deeply, and my emotions seem to run away at times. O Lord, don't let this hour of sorrow turn into despair. Don't let a feeling of resentment or anger sweep away my confidence in Your abiding love. Bring to mind the work of Your Son for my salvation. Give me the confident hope that through Him death has been conquered, and despite what I see and feel, death does not really have the last word. Comfort me with the victory of His resurrection. Roll away the clouds of my emotions that I may be warmed again by the bright light of hope, and that I may walk again in confidence and faith until the glorious day of the resurrection when we shall be reunited in heaven and together walk forever in the new creation, praising and glorifying You forever and ever. In Jesus' name. Amen. (7)

Courage

Lord God, You have called Your servants to ventures of which we cannot see the ending, by paths as yet untrodden, through perils unknown. Give us faith to go out with good courage, not knowing where we go but only that Your hand is leading us and Your love supporting us; through Jesus Christ, Your Son, our Lord. Amen. (8)

Courage

O Lord, with the prophet of old I confess that "my groans are many, and my heart is faint" (Lamentations 1:22). The perplexity of my sorrow, the trials and difficulties that seem to swirl around me—these seem to rob me of my courage. Where will I find the strength and courage to face the days that are ahead? With what little I have left I come to You. Heavenly Father, don't turn me away. "I lift up my eyes. . . . From where does my help come? My help comes from the LORD, who made heaven and earth" (Psalm 121:1, 2). Human help and wisdom are not enough. Bring me to consider not only Your almighty power, but Your loving heart that goes out in compassion to Your children. Revive and refresh me with Your promise to give power to the fainthearted and strength to those who have no might. Give me endurance to run the course that You have set before me. Help me find courage in the knowledge that You hold my past, my present, and my future safely in Your almighty hands. All this I pray in Your Son, Jesus' name. Amen. (9)

Faithfulness and Strength

Father, as You helped Your Son as He walked the way of sorrows carrying His cross, comfort and strengthen me as I bear my cross. Keep me from losing faith in this time of grief, and increase my trust in You even more. Help me believe that You are at work through this trial, and cause me to remember "that the sufferings of this present time are not worth comparing with the glory that is to be revealed" (Romans 8:18). I pray in Jesus' name. Amen. (10)

Fear

Dear heavenly Father, be my guide and comforter. Help me to be content in knowing You and Your love. Be near me when I suffer the "whys" of life. Assure me of Your constant love and care for me. Continue to warm me with Your love in Christ as I face the challenges ahead. In His name. Amen. (11)

For a Thankful Heart

O Lord, the attitude of my heart is a mess. My loss is so fresh and keen that thoughts of gratitude are hard to find at this time. And yet I know that I do indeed have much reason to be thankful even now. In Your great goodness You gave me the very loved one whose death I now mourn and through whom my life was blessed in so many ways. Through him (her) You gave me love and joy and companionship. In great mercy You brought (*name*), whom I cherished, into Your kingdom through Holy Baptism and made him (her) an heir of eternal life. You also sustained him (her) in faith in Jesus Christ, our Savior and Redeemer. Help me ever to remember Your great goodness and to ponder on that more even than on my loss. O God of love, restore to me the joy of my salvation and give me a thankful heart that recognizes, cherishes, and acknowledges Your many blessings. And with a grateful heart grant me also, in due time, healing for my sorrow. In Jesus' name. Amen. (12)

For God's Hand

Friends have offered me their shoulders to cry on and their arms to lean on, yet in my distress, Lord, I am in great need of Your strong and sure hand. Hold me firmly and securely, and let me always feel Your nearness and love, Your care and concern for me in my bereavement. Keep me from despondency and despair of Your help and mercy. Reach out Your hand and guide me in the gloom and shadows that envelope me now because of my sorrow. Graciously lead me on paths of love and kindness back to brighter and better days. And when I falter, because I know I will, do not reject me or forsake me in my weakness, but support me and lift me up again. Hear my prayer in Jesus' name. Amen. (13)

In the hour of trial, Jesus, plead for me
Lest by base denial I depart from Thee.
When Thou see'st me waver, with a look recall
Nor for fear or favor suffer me to fall.

Should Thy mercy send me sorrow, toil, and woe,
Or should pain attend me on my path below,
Grant that I may never fail Thy hand to see;
Grant that I may ever cast my care on Thee. Amen.

(TLH 516:1, 3)

For the Parents of a Stillborn Child, Miscarriage, or Death Shortly after Birth

O Lord God, Your ways are often hidden, unsearchable, and beyond our understanding. For reasons beyond our knowing You have turned the hopes of these parents from joy to sadness, and now You desire that in humble faith we bow before Your ordering of these events. You are the Lord. You do what You know to be good. In their hour of sorrow, comfort them with your life-giving Word, for the sake of Jesus Christ, Your Son, our Lord. Amen. (14)

For Understanding

O God, my eyes are filled with tears of grief. My sorrow has dimmed my vision. Your ways seem dark, mysterious, and unreasonable. Enlighten my understanding that I can perceive that Your ways are always for our good because they lead us heavenward and to You. Instruct me with Your Word that I would not forget Your loving concern for the eternal welfare of all your children, including my loved one and me. I thank You for the gift of Holy Baptism by which we were declared to be Your own dear children. Keep me and strengthen me in this faith by Your almighty power! Help me to remember that where there is dawn, there is also the dark of night, and yet a new morning is sure to come again. Let the pattern You have given us in nature be for me a calm in the face of my turmoil, that turmoil may give way to peace and trust in Your abiding love. In Jesus' name I pray. Amen. (15)

Guilt

Oh, God, Your Word speaks to me. Psalm 40:2 says, "He drew me up from the pit of destruction, out of the miry bog, and set my feet upon a rock, making my steps secure." My feet were definitely in the miry bog today, Lord. I was frustrated and became angry, but the worst part of it was that I let my loved one see my anger. Forgive me, Lord, and help me forgive myself. Be with me as I continue to care for those who rely on me, and help me to always set my feet upon a rock, especially the rock of Your salvation, Jesus Christ, our Lord. Amen. (16)

The Holidays

Heavenly Father, our family had wonderful holidays together in the past. Now after (*name's*) death, I am having a hard time preparing for this occasion. Our memories of the past are precious and heartwarming, but it's not the same anymore. Help us keep a spiritual perspective on this special occasion and on the relationships we still have with one another. I pray that this holiday will be a time to cherish forever as we create new memories to treasure in our hearts. Bless us with Your love and peace. In Jesus' name I pray. Amen. (17)

Mercy

Almighty and everlasting God, You are always more ready to hear us than we are to pray, and always ready to give more than we either ask or deserve to receive. Pour down on us the abundance of Your mercy, forgiving us those things of which our conscience is afraid, and giving us those good things we are not worthy to ask but through the merits and mediation of Your Son, our Lord, Jesus Christ. Amen. (18)

Peace

Lord God, heavenly Father, You sent Your Son to be the Prince of Peace and to give us true and lasting peace in the forgiveness of sins. Grant me Your peace, the peace the world cannot give, and help me live by faith, to trust in You for all things, to forgive others as You have forgiven me, and to rest confidently in Your love. In Jesus' name. Amen. (19)

For Peace

Almighty and most merciful God, You bring us through suffering and death with our Lord Jesus Christ to enter with Him into eternal glory. Grant us grace at all times to acknowledge and accept Your holy and gracious will, to remain in true faith, and to find peace and joy in the resurrection of the dead, and of the glory of everlasting life; through Jesus Christ, Your Son, our Lord. Amen. (20)

Of a Widow

Blessed Lord and beloved Savior, comfort me, Your poor handmaiden, especially in this time of grief and sorrow and such terrible bereavement. You have given me an image of Yourself in the person of my dear husband, whom

You have now taken from me to Yourself in heaven. Oh, how my feelings overwhelm me, and I am so alone! Lord, help me! You are the One who brought me to my husband and united me to him as one flesh. Under You alone, he was my head, my protector, my companion in this world, my friend, and my greatest earthly joy. Indeed, my entire life—my body, mind and spirit—has been intertwined with his. Now that death has parted us, who shall be my helper? I am overcome, and very nearly undone, with loneliness and fear, with mourning, and with anxiety for the future.

Dear Lord Jesus, I do not desire to mourn like those who have no hope. Your Word and Spirit teach me that my help, at all times, comes from You. Forgive me for my misplaced trust in the strength and glory of man. Cleanse me of my sinful worries and concerns, when I sink into doubt, as though You had not conquered death and risen from the dead. Lord, I do believe, but I need You every day and night to help my unbelief. Give me the faith and confidence to seek You where You may be found, within Your holy Church, in the preaching of Your sweet Gospel, and in the Supper of Your true body and true blood. Bring me joyfully and often into that great banquet of Your kingdom, which has no end. In that sure and certain hope, give me strength to face the long and difficult days ahead. Enable me to make wise decisions and to deal with so many new responsibilities. Bless my efforts and correct all my errors. And as I entrust my days and burdens to Your care, grant to me each night a peaceful and quiet sleep, until I shall also fall asleep in You and live forever in Your presence; through Jesus Christ, Your Son, my Lord. Amen. (21)

Of a Widower

Father of mercy and God of all comfort, my only help in all my need, You give and take away according to Your wisdom. You bring down the proud and raise up those whom You have humbled. I cry to You now out of the depths of my sadness, with groans of misery too deep for words, because, through temporal death, You have taken from my side the dear woman whom You gave to be with me. My loss is great, for she has been the delight of my eyes, my true companion, the glory of my house, the one in whom my heart could safely trust regarding all that concerns my earthly welfare.

Lord, look upon my tears, consider my agony of heart and mind and soul, and forgive me all my sin. Do not leave me in despair. You have said, "It is not good that the man should be alone" (Genesis 2:18), yet I am now bereft of my helpmate; I am alone and miserable. Comfort me with Your gracious presence, for the fear in my heart is great. Therefore, teach me by Your Spirit through Word and Sacrament that You are with me and have not left me without consolation.

I confess that, as a husband, I have been a poor reflection of that dear Savior, Jesus Christ. But do not allow my failings to give the devil any foothold in my life. I pray to You in all humility, in repentance and with faith in Your forgiveness: prevent me from becoming lost in my misery. Nor let me falter, in my grief, in those other vocations and responsibilities that remain to me. Enable me to serve my family and neighbor faithfully, even as You continue to serve and protect me. Into Your hands, O Lord, I commend myself entirely; let me never come to ruin. Be my comfort, my shield and strength, my fortress and strong tower, my help and constant companion, that I may praise You for Your faithfulness unto all eternity; through Christ, my Lord. Amen. (22)

Prayer to Accept God's Will

O God of grace and mercy, I thank You for Your loving-kindness shown to all Your servants who, having finished their course in faith, now rest from their labors. Grant me grace to say with a believing heart, "Thy will be done," and know that Your will, though often hidden, is good and gracious. Strengthen me through Your Word and Sacraments for that day when You will call me to Yourself, that I may also be faithful unto death, joyfully receive the crown of eternal life, and join the whole company of heaven to live with You forever. Amen. (23)

Strength

Dear heavenly Father, the burden of grief is heavy, and my strength is all but gone. It all seems more than I can bear. Do not allow me, I pray, to be crushed altogether. Do not let Satan exploit my weakness by undermining my faith and shaking my trust in You. Almighty God, You are the source of all strength and power, and You have promised Your children strength sufficient for each day. Stand by me now, I pray, and strengthen me with Your power in the face of my grief—the power of Jesus' resurrection. Sustain me with the bread of life, Your blessed Word, so that I do not grow faint or collapse, but may meet the heavy demands that have been placed upon me, and adjust to the situation which this loss and my sorrow has brought me. In Jesus, my Savior's name I ask it. Amen. (24)

For Those Who Suffer

I implore You to hear me, O God, for all those worn by illness, all who are wronged and oppressed, the weary and heavy-laden, the aged and the dying, the poor and the lonely, all who are suffering for righteousness' sake, that they may be strengthened by Your might, consoled by Your love, and cherished by Your Fatherly pity; through Jesus Christ, Your Son, our Lord. Amen. (25)

The Lord's Prayer

Our Father who art in heaven, hallowed be Thy name, Thy kingdom come, Thy will be done on earth as it is in heaven. Give us this day our daily bread; and forgive us our trespasses as we forgive those who trespass against us; and lead us not into temptation, but deliver us from evil. For Thine is the kingdom and the power and the glory forever and ever. Amen.

BLESSINGS and PRAYERS
at the APPROACH of DEATH

MEDITATIONS
and COMFORT

Depart in Peace

Lord, now You are letting Your servant depart in peace, according to Your word; for my eyes have seen Your salvation that You have prepared in the presence of all peoples, a light for revelation to the Gentiles, and for glory to Your people Israel.

—Luke 2:29–32

Most people pray for a peaceful death, that is, a death where there is no pain or suffering. Simeon tells of a different kind of peaceful death.

Imagine waiting in the temple year after year for the Savior to appear. Then, there He is—a 40-day-old infant in the arms of His mother, Mary. What joy and peace—peace that reigns between heaven and earth because God has become flesh to take away the sins of the world.

Simeon may now depart in peace; he has seen the Lord's salvation; he has held the Lord in his arms. So have you. You have taken the Lord's body in your hands and placed it in your mouth; you have taken the cup and tipped His life-giving blood to your lips. You have touched the Lord and tasted that He is good. He has given you the peace of heaven in His body and blood. "Depart in peace," says the pastor, as you leave the table of the Lord, and you do.

Your death is the entrance into a life that never ends. When you close your eyes in death, you will be with Christ and His angels and archangels and all the company of heaven.

Lord, now let this, Your servant, depart in peace.

29
Comfort

God Cares

....

Turn to me and be gracious to me, for I am lonely and afflicted. The troubles of my heart are enlarged; bring me out of my distresses. Consider my affliction and my trouble, and forgive all my sins.

—Psalm 25:16–18

The world is full of people in suffering and pain, many of them afflicted far more than I. How can I be sure that God even knows about me, much less looks upon me?

"I have called you by name, you are Mine," the Lord guarantees (Isaiah 43:1). By name He called Adam, Noah, Abram, Jeremiah, Mary and Joseph, the disciples, Mary Magdalene—and He stayed by them all their days. Likewise, He promises His abiding presence to every troubled and distressed soul.

But shouldn't I hide from God because of all my rebellious thoughts, all my sins?

If it were not for Christ and His sacrificial love on Calvary, I should tremble in God's presence, for I am unholy because of my sin and my shame. But God's Son died an unholy and shameful death, becoming sin for me, that I might be holy and whole in Him. Jesus touches me with His healing hand, He draws me to His loving heart, and He blots out all my sins.

Even if the pain continues, my burden is made lighter because I am at peace with God. His love and power will see me through every difficulty and bring a ray of light into the darkest night. Therefore, I can rest and sleep; He is watching over me with His tender care every hour of my sickness.

God's Precious Saints

Precious in the sight of the LORD is the death of His saints. O LORD, I am Your servant; I am Your servant, the son of Your maidservant. You have loosed my bonds.

—Psalm 116:15–16

How is death precious to the Lord? God is the God of life. He breathed His own Spirit into man so that we live as the unique bearers of His image. God did not create this world with death. Death is a result of sin, and sin is in opposition to this God of life. Does God really look at death as precious?

But the verse says, "the death of His saints." It is not death that is precious to God, but His saints. Death is an enemy of God. It is the result of sin. Sin leads to death, but death swallows up sin. After we die, we no longer sin. The unfaithfulness of our hearts, the harshness of our words, and the selfishness of our actions are all dead. Sin has no more power. The old man that began to drown in Baptism is now swallowed up forever, and there is only the new life that we have in Christ. This is why Baptism is compared to dying; in Baptism, sin and the devil's hold over us dies. At our earthly death, sins can no longer be committed.

In our Lord's death, He took on the true death of hell that should have been ours. On the cross, the enemies of God were truly destroyed, the devil's plan backfired, and death and sin swallowed up themselves. Through His death, Jesus has loosed the bonds of your death. You are free from the death of hell, and your own passing is but a brief slumber that takes you to the arms of Jesus Christ. Because He endured your death—taking it upon Himself—you have true life and will never truly die.

Therefore, just as your death is His, so His life is yours. When God raised Jesus up, He raised you up and made this resurrection yours in your Baptism. And He has continued to assure you of this life. When you eat and drink Christ's body and blood, this living God unites Himself again to you, forgiving your sin, and rejuvenating you, even as your body appears to be failing. Your body, broken by death, will be restored by this body of God and will live forever, the culmination of the life of faith that you have in Christ. In these days and hours before death, look to Christ who died the full death of hell so that you will live a new life. His resurrected body and blood are yours. His promise is yours. He has loosed your bonds forever. Precious, indeed, in the sight of the Lord is the death of His saints.

Lord, Let at Last
Your Angels Come

After this I looked, and behold, a great multitude that no one could number, from every nation, from all tribes and peoples and languages, standing before the throne and before the Lamb, clothed in white robes, with palm branches in their hands, and crying out with a loud voice, "Salvation belongs to our God who sits on the throne, and to the Lamb!" And all the angels were standing around the throne and around the elders and the four living creatures, and they fell on their faces before the throne and worshiped God, saying, "Amen! Blessing and glory and wisdom and thanksgiving and honor and power and might be to our God forever and ever! Amen."

–Revelation 7:9–12

Every time that you received the body of and blood of the Lord at the Lord's Supper, you entered heaven. Jesus Christ, the crucified, risen, and ascended Lord, gave you in His body and blood a taste of heaven right now, even now, here on earth.

As you prepared to receive the Lord's Supper, you sang, "Therefore with angels and archangels and all the company of heaven, we laud and magnify Your holy name, evermore praising you and saying." In these words, you acknowledged that in this Holy Meal you joined with angels and archangels and all the saints, that is, with Christ and all who are with Him in heaven. Heaven came to earth in Jesus, and you are invited to enter heaven right now, even now, here on earth.

Throughout your life and even now, you worship the Lamb because He was slain and raised again. His sprinkled blood has made you and all creation clean. By His wounds you have been healed, and the food He gives you at this heavenly feast is His body broken in death, His blood poured out for the forgiveness of your sins.

Your Lord invites you to the Lord's Table, however burdened by sin and guilt and shame. You are battle-weary from fighting the good fight. With St. Paul, you long to be with Christ, for you know that there, before the throne and before the Lamb, you will join the great multitude that no one can number, clothed in white robes, with palm branches in their hands. You long to join them, without the noise of sin and death, so you can cry, "Salvation belongs to our God who sits on the throne, and to the Lamb!" You are ready to join the angels and saints before the throne of the

Lamb and worship God, saying, "Amen! Blessing and glory and wisdom and thanksgiving and honor and power and might be to our God forever and ever! Amen."

You have suffered with Christ. You have borne the burden of the day. It is time to commend you to the Lamb.

32
Assurance

Now I Lay Me Down to Sleep

But we do not want you to be un-informed, brothers, about those who are asleep, that you may not grieve as others do who have no hope. For since we believe that Jesus died and rose again, even so, through Jesus, God will bring with Him those who have fallen asleep. For this we declare to you by a word from the Lord, that we who are alive, who are left until the coming of the Lord, will not precede those who have fallen asleep. For the Lord

Himself will descend from heaven with a cry of command, with the voice of an archangel, and with the sound of the trumpet of God. And the dead in Christ will rise first. Then we who are alive, who are left, will be caught up together with them in the clouds to meet the Lord in the air, and so we will always be with the Lord. Therefore encourage one another with these words.

—1 Thessalonians 4:13–18

There is probably nothing in life that we fear more than death. This fear is demonstrated in the fact that we avoid the noun *death* and the verb *die*. In medical circles, a patient doesn't die; instead, he or she "expires." In daily conversation, we often employ the euphemism "passed away" rather than say that a person has died.

Jesus explained why we need not fear death when He said to Martha, "I am the resurrection and the life. Whoever believes in Me, though he die, yet shall he live, and everyone who lives and believes in Me shall never die" (John 11:25–26). For those who trust in Jesus for forgiveness and life, death is but the door through which they enter into an even better life. By His death and triumphant resurrection, Jesus has made complete payment for all sins.

Paul writes about "the dead in Christ" (1 Thessalonians

4:16), who are "asleep": "We do not want you to be uninformed, brothers, about those who are asleep. . . . God will bring with Him those who have fallen asleep. . . . We who are alive . . . will not precede those who have fallen asleep" (vv. 13–15).

It's a pleasant experience to fall asleep, especially if we are tired after a day of hard work. Actually, the bad experience is to be unable to sleep, to toss and turn as we wait for morning to come. To sleep is pleasant, and to awaken from sleep refreshed and strengthened is one of the most pleasant experiences of all.

When St. Paul refers to death as a sleep, he is saying in a very powerful way that you who believe in Jesus do not have to be afraid of death any more than you are afraid of falling asleep at the end of the day. That's why many parents taught their children at an early age to pray at bedtime: "Now I lay me down to sleep. I pray the Lord my soul to keep; and if I die before I wake, I pray the Lord my soul to take; and this I ask for Jesus' sake."

Do not fear death, because your faith in Christ assures you of the gift of eternal life. Jesus Himself said this in the best-known Bible verse of all when He declared, "For God so loved the world, that He gave His only Son, that whoever believes in Him should not perish but have eternal life" (John 3:16).

St. Paul speaks of the Last Day, the day when you and all the saints will receive that eternal life, as a day of celebration: "The Lord Himself will descend from heaven with a cry of command, with the voice of an archangel, and with the sound of the trumpet of God. And the dead in Christ will rise first. Then we who are alive, who are left, will be caught up together with them in the clouds to meet the Lord in the air, and so we will always be with the Lord" (1 Thessalonians 4:16–17).

"And so we will always be with the Lord"! We can't really imagine or comprehend what eternal life will be like.

One Sunday School youngster did a pretty good job of summarizing the joy of eternal life when she was asked to define heaven. "Heaven," said the little girl, "is when it's Christmas every day!" What a precious and accurate summary! Remember the days of your childhood, when you couldn't wait for Christmas to come? And when that great day finally arrived, we wished that the joy of Christmas would last forever. And it will!

> All praise to Thee, my God, this night
> For all the blessings of the light.
> Keep me, O keep me, King of kings,
> Beneath Thine own almighty wings. (*LSB* 883:1)

The Cup of Salvation

I am already being poured out as a drink offering, and the time of my departure has come. I have fought the good fight, I have finished the race, I have kept the faith. Henceforth there is laid up for me the crown of righteousness, which the Lord, the righteous judge, will award to me on that Day, and not only to me but also to all who have loved His appearing.

—2 Timothy 4:6–8

The Lord chose you and made you His own in Baptism. He gave you faith and sustains your life in Christ. His eyes saw you before you were born, and He sees you now. The Lord guards this day for you, keeping you in His care.

You have a crown of righteousness earned by the life, death, and resurrection of our Savior, Jesus Christ. The righteous Judge, God Himself, finds no wrong in you, for you are His child, washed clean and fully restored to Him. All fears will pass and all your tears will be wiped away.

Before Christ poured out His soul to death, He was transfigured, giving us a glimpse of our own future. You, too, will be glorified in your body. Christ rose in triumph to prepare a special place for you and for all who love Him. You, too, will be raised to live in a place without pain, loss, or fear, where you will live with all the saints in His paradise forever.

34
Faith

The Dying Person
Prays for a Blessed End

It is enough; now, O Lord, take away my life, for I am no better than my fathers.

—1 Kings 19:4

In the Old Testament, when a person brought an offering to the Lord, it had to be voluntary, not a compulsory offering. This rule applies also to our dying: we must not die with displeasure or by constraint or with grumbling and disgust, but we should learn from God's Word, while still in good health, that there is glory prepared for us in the life to come, learn about the crown, the white robe, and the joy that we shall obtain after this life. We should also acquaint ourselves with the Way that leads to this glory, which is Jesus Christ, in order that we may persevere in faith until death.

On the approach of the hour that God has appointed for our departure from this world, we should lift up our eyes unto heaven with joy and beg God for a blessed end. This may be done in the following manner: We may commit our body and soul to God, continually think of our dear Savior, pray fervently, and thus await our last hour. At the same time we may call on God to grant us a quiet, gentle, rational, and blessed end. If unbecoming actions occur occasionally, those gathered at the bedside of a dying person need not worry too much about this, as the dying may be less sensible of it than they think, and meanwhile the dying remains in sweet communion with his beloved Redeemer.

35
Assurance

The Lord Is Waiting for You

> He will swallow up death forever; and the Lord God will wipe away tears from all faces, and the reproach of His people He will take away from

all the earth, for the LORD has spoken.
It will be said on that day, "Behold,
this is our God; we have waited for
Him, that He might save us. This is
the LORD; we have waited for Him; let
us be glad and rejoice in His salvation."

—Isaiah 25:8–9

You have waited for the Lord. You have endured the weight of sin in this life, and have persevered in faith in your Lord Jesus Christ. The fulfillment of His promise to wipe away all your tears is nearer now than it once was.

What lies ahead is unknown to you. You do not know the way. Even now, look to your Good Shepherd to lead you from this wilderness, across the deep river Jordan, into the promised land.

I tell you, Christian, you will walk through on dry ground. Having already died with Christ in your Baptism, you will not taste death, but will pass through death to life. Death is swallowed up forever. His blood has already paid the wages of your sin.

As you journey this last stretch, through the valley of death, He is attentive to you and tender. Like a lamb you are borne on His shoulders. Soon you will see Him face-to-face. This is the Lord. You have waited for Him; He is now waiting for you.

SELECTED HYMNS

Before the Throne of God Above

Before the throne of God above
    I have a strong, a perfect plea:
A great High Priest, whose name is Love,
    Who ever lives and pleads for me.

When Satan tempts me to despair,
    And tells me of the guilt within,
Upward I look, and see Him there
    Who made an end of all my sin.

Behold Him there! The risen Lamb!
    My perfect, spotless righteousness,
The great unchangeable I AM,
    The King of glory and of grace! (*LSB* 574:1, 3, 5)

Christ Is the World's Redeemer

Christ is the world's Redeemer,
    The lover of the pure,
The font of heav'nly wisdom,
    Our trust and hope secure,
The armor of His soldiers,
    The Lord of earth and sky,
Our health while we are living,
    Our life when we shall die.

Christ has our host surrounded
    With clouds of martyrs bright,
Who wave their palms in triumph
    And fire us for the fight.
Then Christ the cross ascended
    To save a world undone
And, suff'ring for the sinful,
    Our full redemption won.

Down through the realm of darkness
    He strode in victory,
And at the hour appointed
    He rose triumphantly.
And now, to heav'n ascended,
    He sits upon the throne
Whence He had ne'er departed,
    His Father's and His own.

Glory to God the Father,
    The unbegotten One,
All honor be to Jesus,
    His sole-begotten Son,
And to the Holy Spirit—
    The perfect Trinity.
Let all the worlds give answer:
    Amen! So let it be. (*LSB* 539)

God's Own Child, I'll Gladly Say It

Death, you cannot end my gladness:
 I am baptized into Christ!
When I die, I leave all sadness
 To inherit paradise!
Though I lie in dust and ashes
Faith's assurance brightly flashes:
 Baptism has the strength divine
 To make life immortal mine.

There is nothing worth comparing
 To this lifelong comfort sure!
Open-eyed my grave is staring:
 Even there I'll sleep secure.
Though my flesh awaits its raising,
Still my soul continues praising:
 I am baptized into Christ;
 I'm a child of paradise! (*LSB* 594:4–5)

I Heard the Voice of Jesus Say

I heard the voice of Jesus say,
    "Come unto Me and rest;
Lay down, thou weary one, lay down
    Thy head upon My breast."
I came to Jesus as I was,
    So weary, worn, and sad;
I found in Him a resting place,
    And He has made me glad.

I heard the voice of Jesus say,
    "Behold, I freely give
The living water; thirsty one,
    Stoop down and drink and live."
I came to Jesus, and I drank
    Of that life-giving stream;
My thirst was quenched, my soul revived,
    And now I live in Him.

I heard the voice of Jesus say,
    "I am this dark world's light.
Look unto Me; thy morn shall rise
    And all thy day be bright."
I looked to Jesus, and I found
    In Him my star, my sun;
And in that light of life I'll walk
    Till trav'ling days are done. (*LSB* 699:1–3)

I'm But a Stranger Here

I'm but a stranger here,
    Heav'n is my home;
Earth is a desert drear,
    Heav'n is my home.
Danger and sorrow stand
Round me on ev'ry hand;
Heav'n is my fatherland,
    Heav'n is my home.

What though the tempest rage,
    Heav'n is my home;
Short is my pilgrimage,
    Heav'n is my home;
And time's wild wintry blast
Soon shall be overpast;
I shall reach home at last,
    Heav'n is my home.

Therefore I murmur not,
    Heav'n is my home;
Whate'er my earthly lot,
    Heav'n is my home;
And I shall surely stand
There at my Lord's right hand;
Heav'n is my fatherland,
    Heav'n is my home. (*LSB* 748)

In Peace and Joy I Now Depart

In peace and joy I now depart
    Since God so wills it.
Serene and confident my heart;
    Stillness fills it.
For the Lord has promised me
That death is but a slumber.

Christ Jesus brought this gift to me,
    My faithful Savior,
Whom You have made my eyes to see
    By Your favor.
Now I know He is my life,
My friend when I am dying.

You sent the people of the earth
    Their great salvation;
Your invitation summons forth
    Ev'ry nation
By Your holy, precious Word,
In ev'ry place resounding.

Christ is the hope and saving light
    Of those in blindness;
He guides and comforts those in night
    By His kindness.
For Your people Israel
In Him find joy and glory. (*LSB* 938)

Lord, Thee I Love with All My Heart

Lord, Thee I love with all my heart;
I pray Thee, ne'er from me depart,
　　With tender mercy cheer me.
Earth has no pleasure I would share.
Yea, heav'n itself were void and bare
　　If Thou, Lord, wert not near me.
And should my heart for sorrow break,
My trust in Thee can nothing shake.
　　Thou art the portion I have sought;
　　Thy precious blood my soul has bought.
Lord Jesus Christ, my God and Lord, my God and Lord,
Forsake me not! I trust Thy Word.

Yea, Lord, 'twas Thy rich bounty gave
My body, soul, and all I have
　　In this poor life of labor.
Lord, grant that I in ev'ry place
May glorify Thy lavish grace
　　And help and serve my neighbor.
Let no false doctrine me beguile;
Let Satan not my soul defile.
　　Give strength and patience unto me
　　To bear my cross and follow Thee.
Lord Jesus Christ, my God and Lord, my God and Lord,
In death Thy comfort still afford.

Lord, let at last Thine angels come,
To Abr'ham's bosom bear me home,
    That I may die unfearing;
And in its narrow chamber keep
My body safe in peaceful sleep
    Until Thy reappearing.
And then from death awaken me,
That these mine eyes with joy may see,
    O Son of God, Thy glorious face,
    My Savior and my fount of grace.
Lord Jesus Christ, my prayer attend, my prayer attend,
And I will praise Thee without end. (*LSB* 708)

Once in the Blest Baptismal Waters

Once in the blest baptismal waters
    I put on Christ and made Him mine;
Now numbered with God's sons and daughters,
    I share His peace and love divine.

O God, for Jesus' sake I pray
Your peace may bless my dying day.

His body and His blood I've taken
    In His blest Supper, feast divine;
Now I shall never be forsaken,
    For I am His, and He is mine.

O God, for Jesus' sake I pray
Your peace may bless my dying day.

And thus I live in God contented
    And die without a thought of fear;
My soul has to God's plans consented,
    For through His Son my faith is clear.

O God, for Jesus' sake I pray
Your peace may bless my dying day. (*LSB* 598)

SELECTED PSALMS

Assurance

Psalm 16

¹ Preserve me, O God, for in You I take refuge.

² I say to the Lord, "You are my Lord;
   I have no good apart from You."

³ As for the saints in the land, they are the excellent ones,
   in whom is all my delight.

⁴ The sorrows of those who run after another god shall multiply;
   their drink offerings of blood I will not pour out
   or take their names on my lips.

⁵ The Lord is my chosen portion and my cup;
   You hold my lot.

⁶ The lines have fallen for me in pleasant places;
   indeed, I have a beautiful inheritance.

⁷ I bless the Lord who gives me counsel;
   in the night also my heart instructs me.

⁸ I have set the Lord always before me;
   because He is at my right hand, I shall not be shaken.

⁹ Therefore my heart is glad, and my whole being rejoices;
   my flesh also dwells secure.

¹⁰ For You will not abandon my soul to Sheol,
   or let Your holy one see corruption.

¹¹ You make known to me the path of life;
   in Your presence there is fullness of joy;
   at Your right hand are pleasures forevermore.

Comfort

Psalm 17:1-9

¹ Hear a just cause, O Lord; attend to my cry!
Give ear to my prayer from lips free of deceit!
² From Your presence let my vindication come!
Let Your eyes behold the right!
³ You have tried my heart, You have visited me by night,
You have tested me, and You will find nothing;
I have purposed that my mouth will not transgress.
⁴ With regard to the works of man, by the word of Your lips
I have avoided the ways of the violent.
⁵ My steps have held fast to Your paths;
my feet have not slipped.
⁶ I call upon You, for You will answer me, O God;
incline Your ear to me; hear my words.
⁷ Wondrously show Your steadfast love,
O Savior of those who seek refuge
from their adversaries at Your right hand.
⁸ Keep me as the apple of Your eye;
hide me in the shadow of Your wings,
⁹ from the wicked who do me violence,
my deadly enemies who surround me.

The Lord Is My Shepherd

Psalm 23

¹ The LORD is my shepherd; I shall not want.
  ² He makes me lie down in green pastures.
He leads me beside still waters.
  ³ He restores my soul.
He leads me in paths of righteousness
    for His name's sake.
⁴ Even though I walk through the valley of the shadow
  of death,
    I will fear no evil,
for You are with me;
      Your rod and Your staff,
      they comfort me.
⁵ You prepare a table before me
    in the presence of my enemies;
You anoint my head with oil;
    my cup overflows.
⁶ Surely goodness and mercy shall follow me
    all the days of my life,
and I shall dwell in the house of the LORD
        forever.

Confidence

Psalm 27:1–5

[1] The LORD is my light and my salvation;
    whom shall I fear?
The LORD is the stronghold of my life;
    of whom shall I be afraid?
[2] When evildoers assail me
    to eat up my flesh,
my adversaries and foes,
    it is they who stumble and fall.
[3] Though an army encamp against me,
    my heart shall not fear;
though war arise against me,
    yet I will be confident.
[4] One thing have I asked of the LORD,
    that will I seek after:
that I may dwell in the house of the LORD
    all the days of my life,
to gaze upon the beauty of the LORD
    and to inquire in His temple.
[5] For He will hide me in His shelter
    in the day of trouble;
He will conceal me under the cover of His tent;
    He will lift me high upon a rock.

Commendation of the Dying
Psalm 31:5-8

⁵ Into Your hand I commit my spirit;
>   You have redeemed me, O Lᴏʀᴅ, faithful God.
⁶ I hate those who pay regard to worthless idols,
>   but I trust in the Lᴏʀᴅ.
⁷ I will rejoice and be glad in Your steadfast love,
>   because You have seen my affliction;
>   You have known the distress of my soul,
⁸ and You have not delivered me into the hand of the
    enemy;
>   You have set my feet in a broad place.

Courage
Psalm 31:9-15, 23-24

⁹ Be gracious to me, O Lᴏʀᴅ, for I am in distress;
>   my eye is wasted from grief;
>   my soul and my body also.
¹⁰ For my life is spent with sorrow,
>   and my years with sighing;
>   my strength fails because of my iniquity,
>   and my bones waste away.
¹¹ Because of all my adversaries I have become a
    reproach,
>   especially to my neighbors,
>   and an object of dread to my acquaintances;

those who see me in the street flee from me.
¹² I have been forgotten like one who is dead;
I have become like a broken vessel.
¹³ For I hear the whispering of many—
terror on every side!—
as they scheme together against me,
as they plot to take my life.
¹⁴ But I trust in You, O Lord;
I say, "You are my God."
¹⁵ My times are in Your hand;
rescue me from the hand of my enemies and
from my persecutors!
²³ Love the Lord, all you His saints!
The Lord preserves the faithful
but abundantly repays the one who acts in pride.
²⁴ Be strong, and let your heart take courage,
all you who wait for the Lord!

Deliverance
Psalm 34:12, 17–19

¹² What man is there who desires life
and loves many days, that he may see good?
¹⁷ When the righteous cry for help, the Lord hears
and delivers them out of all their troubles.
¹⁸ The Lord is near to the brokenhearted
and saves the crushed in spirit.
¹⁹ Many are the afflictions of the righteous,
but the Lord delivers him out of them all.

God Is My Strength
Psalm 73:26–28

26 My flesh and my heart may fail,
  but God is the strength of my heart and my
  portion forever.
27 For behold, those who are far from You shall perish;
  You put an end to everyone who is unfaithful
  to You.
28 But for me it is good to be near God;
  I have made the Lord God my refuge,
  that I may tell of all Your works.

Comforting the Bereaved
Psalm 90

1 Lord, You have been our dwelling place
  in all generations.
2 Before the mountains were brought forth,
  or ever You had formed the earth and the world,
  from everlasting to everlasting You are God.
3 You return man to dust
  and say, "Return, O children of man!"
4 For a thousand years in Your sight
  are but as yesterday when it is past,
  or as a watch in the night.
5 You sweep them away as with a flood; they are like
  a dream,

like grass that is renewed in the morning:

[6] in the morning it flourishes and is renewed;

in the evening it fades and withers.

[7] For we are brought to an end by Your anger;

by Your wrath we are dismayed.

[8] You have set our iniquities before You,

our secret sins in the light of Your presence.

[9] For all our days pass away under Your wrath;

we bring our years to an end like a sigh.

[10] The years of our life are seventy,

or even by reason of strength eighty;

yet their span is but toil and trouble;

they are soon gone, and we fly away.

[11] Who considers the power of Your anger,

and Your wrath according to the fear of You?

[12] So teach us to number our days

that we may get a heart of wisdom.

[13] Return, O Lord! How long?

Have pity on Your servants!

[14] Satisfy us in the morning with Your steadfast love,

that we may rejoice and be glad all our days.

[15] Make us glad for as many days as You have afflicted us,

and for as many years as we have seen evil.

[16] Let Your work be shown to Your servants,

and Your glorious power to their children.

[17] Let the favor of the Lord our God be upon us,

and establish the work of our hands upon us;

yes, establish the work of our hands!

Hope

Psalm 102:11–13

¹¹ My days are like an evening shadow;
　　I wither away like grass.
¹² But You, O Lord, are enthroned forever;
　　You are remembered throughout all generations.
¹³ You will arise and have pity on Zion;
　　it is the time to favor her;
　　the appointed time has come.

I Am Your Servant

Psalm 116:15–19

¹⁵ Precious in the sight of the Lord
　　is the death of His saints.
¹⁶ O Lord, I am Your servant;
　　I am Your servant, the son of Your maidservant.
　　You have loosed my bonds.
¹⁷ I will offer to You the sacrifice of thanksgiving
　　and call on the name of the Lord.
¹⁸ I will pay my vows to the Lord
　　in the presence of all His people,
¹⁹ in the courts of the house of the Lord,
　　in your midst, O Jerusalem.
Praise the Lord!

Consolation and Comfort

Psalm 130:1–8

¹ Out of the depths I cry to You, O Lᴏʀᴅ!
  ² O Lord, hear my voice!
Let Your ears be attentive
    to the voice of my pleas for mercy!
³ If You, O Lᴏʀᴅ, should mark iniquities,
    O Lord, who could stand?
⁴ But with You there is forgiveness,
    that You may be feared.
⁵ I wait for the Lᴏʀᴅ, my soul waits,
    and in His word I hope;
⁶ my soul waits for the Lord
    more than watchmen for the morning,
    more than watchmen for the morning.
⁷ O Israel, hope in the Lᴏʀᴅ!
    For with the Lᴏʀᴅ there is steadfast love,
    and with Him is plentiful redemption.
⁸ And He will redeem Israel
    from all his iniquities.

Selected Scripture Passages

Rest for the Soul

²⁸Come to Me, all who labor and are heavy laden, and I will give you rest. ²⁹Take My yoke upon you, and learn from Me, for I am gentle and lowly in heart, and you will find rest for your souls. ³⁰For My yoke is easy, and My burden is light.

Hope in the Resurrection

¹When the Sabbath was past, Mary Magdalene, Mary the mother of James, and Salome bought spices, so that they might go and anoint Him. ²And very early on the first day of the week, when the sun had risen, they went to the tomb. ³And they were saying to one another, "Who will roll away the stone for us from the entrance of the tomb?" ⁴And looking up, they saw that the stone had been rolled back—it was very large. ⁵And entering the tomb, they saw a young man sitting on the right side, dressed in a white robe, and they were alarmed. ⁶And he said to them, "Do not be alarmed. You seek Jesus of Nazareth, who was crucified. He has risen; He is not here. See the place where they laid Him. ⁷But go, tell His disciples and Peter that He is going before you to Galilee. There you will see Him, just as He told you." ⁸And they went out and fled from the tomb, for trembling and astonishment had seized them, and they said nothing to anyone, for they were afraid.

Jesus Gives Life John 3:16–21

¹⁶For God so loved the world, that He gave His only Son, that whoever believes in Him should not perish but have eternal life. ¹⁷For God did not send His Son into the world to condemn the world, but in order that the world might be saved through Him. ¹⁸Whoever believes in Him is not condemned, but whoever does not believe is condemned already, because he has not believed in the name of the only Son of God. ¹⁹And this is the judgment: the light has come into the world, and people loved the darkness rather than the light because their works were evil. ²⁰For everyone who does wicked things hates the light and does not come to the light, lest his works should be exposed. ²¹But whoever does what is true comes to the light, so that it may be clearly seen that his works have been carried out in God.

Assurance John 6:40

⁴⁰For this is the will of My Father, that everyone who looks on the Son and believes in Him should have eternal life, and I will raise him up on the last day.

Assurance John 10:27–29

²⁷My sheep hear My voice, and I know them, and they follow Me. ²⁸I give them eternal life, and they will never perish, and no one will snatch them out of My hand. ²⁹My Father, who has given them to Me, is greater than all, and no one is able to snatch them out of the Father's hand.

¹Now on the first day of the week Mary Magdalene came to the tomb early, while it was still dark, and saw that the stone had been taken away from the tomb. ²So she ran and went to Simon Peter and the other disciple, the one whom Jesus loved, and said to them, "They have taken the Lord out of the tomb, and we do not know where they have laid Him." ³So Peter went out with the other disciple, and they were going toward the tomb. ⁴Both of them were running together, but the other disciple outran Peter and reached the tomb first. ⁵And stooping to look in, he saw the linen cloths lying there, but he did not go in. ⁶Then Simon Peter came, following him, and went into the tomb. He saw the linen cloths lying there, ⁷and the face cloth, which had been on Jesus' head, not lying with the linen cloths but folded up in a place by itself. ⁸Then the other disciple, who had reached the tomb first, also went in, and he saw and believed; ⁹for as yet they did not understand the Scripture, that He must rise from the dead. ¹⁰Then the disciples went back to their homes.

¹¹But Mary stood weeping outside the tomb, and as she wept she stooped to look into the tomb. ¹²And she saw two angels in white, sitting where the body of Jesus had lain, one at the head and one at the feet. ¹³They said to her, "Woman, why are you weeping?" She said to them, "They have taken away my Lord, and I do not know where they have laid Him." ¹⁴Having said this, she turned around and saw Jesus standing, but she did not know that it was Jesus. ¹⁵Jesus said to her, "Woman, why are you weeping? Whom are you seeking?" Supposing Him to be the gardener, she

said to Him, "Sir, if You have carried Him away, tell me where you have laid Him, and I will take Him away." ¹⁶Jesus said to her, "Mary." She turned and said to Him in Aramaic, "Rabboni!" (which means Teacher). ¹⁷Jesus said to her, "Do not cling to Me, for I have not yet ascended to the Father; but go to My brothers and say to them, 'I am ascending to My Father and your Father, to My God and your God.' " ¹⁸Mary Magdalene went and announced to the disciples, "I have seen the Lord"—and that He had said these things to her.

The Last Day   Revelation 7:9–17
....

⁹After this I looked, and behold, a great multitude that no one could number, from every nation, from all tribes and peoples and languages, standing before the throne and before the Lamb, clothed in white robes, with palm branches in their hands, ¹⁰and crying out with a loud voice, "Salvation belongs to our God who sits on the throne, and to the Lamb!" ¹¹And all the angels were standing around the throne and around the elders and the four living creatures, and they fell on their faces before the throne and worshiped God, ¹²saying, "Amen! Blessing and glory and wisdom and thanksgiving and honor and power and might be to our God forever and ever! Amen."

¹³Then one of the elders addressed me, saying, "Who are these, clothed in white robes, and from where have they come?" ¹⁴I said to him, "Sir, you know." And he said to me, "These are the ones coming out of the great tribulation. They have washed their robes and made them white in the blood of the Lamb.

[15]"Therefore they are before the throne of God,
and serve Him day and night in His temple;
and He who sits on the throne will shelter them
with His presence. [16]They shall hunger
no more, neither thirst anymore;
the sun shall not strike them,
nor any scorching heat.
[17]For the Lamb in the midst of the throne will be their
shepherd,
and He will guide them to springs of living water,
and God will wipe away every tear from their
eyes."

PRAYERS for OURSELVES and OTHERS

They Say I'm Dying

I'm dying. I see it in the helpless look of my doctor's eyes. I hear it in the concerned voices of friends and family. Some are calling and visiting more often now; some are staying away. Cards are propped up all over my room. "Get well soon," they say. I know that will be, but not before I die. I feel the chill of death in my bones and smell it on my breath. Thoughts of death cloud my mind, especially in the dark hours of the night. Sleep is shallow and restless, yet I seem to crave sleep more and more. I am weary and my body aches. My appetite is gone. Each day seems to bring new losses, greater weakness.

Have mercy on me, O Lord. I fear Your judgments, for they are just and true. "The wages of sin is death" (Romans 6:23), and my death is just and well deserved. I am a sinner, from the moment You breathed life into me until the day of my death; I am a child of Adam, doomed to die. My sin is always before me, now more than ever, as I lie on my bed and ponder my life. O Father, how I have sinned against You and those around me! I am ashamed even to admit it. I sometimes try to minimize to others and say, "I've lived a good life," but I know the truth. Every day of my life has been soiled with sin. I am afraid of dying. I fear the unknown; I fear losing hold on my life.

And yet, by Your grace, I am unafraid. Your psalmist says, "Precious in the sight of the LORD is the death of His children" (Psalm 116:15), and the Holy Spirit cries out from heaven, "Blessed are [those] who die in the Lord" (Revelation 14:13). I cling to these words. Your Son Jesus, my

194

Lord, became man to take up my sins and my sinfulness in His own sinless humanity and to bury it all in His perfect death. He embraced me on His cross, and in Him I already am judged and crucified. Grant me to trust this with all my heart!

I dare not plead my good works before You, for they are hopelessly tarnished with sin. I do not plead my piety, nor even the depth of knowledge You have given me from the Holy Scriptures. I plead only the blood of Jesus Christ, Your Lamb who took away the sin of the world. I stand before You clothed only with His righteousness, innocence, and blessedness. He is my Rock; on Him I rest. He is my Redeemer; in Him I am hidden in safety.

I thank You, gracious Lord, for my Baptism. With Your hand and in Your name, You buried me in the death of Your Son. You raised me in His resurrection. You seated me with Him at Your right hand in glory. You made me Your beloved child and opened heaven to me, washing away all my sin. You gave me Your own testimony, that I can face my death with a clear conscience, through the merits of Jesus, my Savior. And You did all this long before I knew even to ask for it. By grace I am saved!

I thank You for the gift of Absolution, those precious words calling out to me, forgiving me, reminding me, urging me to trust Your promises. I thank You for faithful pastors who preached the Word of forgiveness to me. I thank You for the company of the saints, my fellow pilgrims in Your holy Church—for their encouragements, their prayers, their works of mercy, their examples of faithfulness.

I thank You for the body and the blood of Your Son,

Jesus Christ, my Lord. I go to His holy Supper as though I were going to my own death, so that I might go to my death as though going to His holy Supper. Surely, my cup overflows with mercy, and I can depart in peace, according to Your Word.

O Father in heaven, let Your name be hallowed in my death. Grant me to honor You in my dying breath, not that I may earn Your favor, but that those around me, whom I love and for whom Your Son has died, might also fear and trust in You.

Let Your kingdom come, that I may see You face-to-face, and live eternally under the reign of Jesus Christ, my Lord who died for me.

Let Your good and gracious will be done with me. Hinder and put to death the will of the devil, who would plague me with doubt and disbelief; the world, that would lead me to despair; and my own sinful flesh, that would drive me into myself and away from You.

Comfort those around me—my family, my friends, my neighbors, my doctors and nurses and all who care for me, my co-workers, my congregation and pastors. Bless them with Your strength in this time of trial. Remind them that You are the God of the living, whose Son conquered death by His dying and rising. Set the joy of Easter and the open, empty tomb of Jesus before their eyes, and wipe away every tear of grief. Encourage them with the knowledge that those who die in the Lord are not lost, nor are they far away, but they are as near as the Lord Jesus Christ, in whom live all the saints, joined together as one body, as we will see with our own eyes on the Day of Resurrection. Amen. (26)

Teach me to live that I may dread
The grave as little as my bed.
Teach me to die that so I may
Rise glorious at the awe-full day. (*LSB* 883:3)

After a Loved One Has Died

O God the Father, fountain and source of all blessing, we give thanks that You have kept our brother (sister)
(*name*) in the faith and have now taken him (her) to Yourself. Comfort us with Your holy Word, and give us strength
that when our last hour comes we may peacefully fall asleep
in You; through Jesus Christ Amen. (27)

As Death Approaches a Loved One

O Lord, one whom I love and care about is dying. Yet
Your love of him (her) is still greater, for You have redeemed
him (her) with the precious blood of Your Son. If it be Your
will that he (she) should pass out of this mortal life, receive
him (her) to Yourself in glory. If this be his (her) last night
on earth, let Your holy angels take him (her) into Your presence, where there is no more pain and suffering and sin, but
fullness of joy forevermore. Wash him (her) of all sin, and
accept him (her) for Jesus' sake. Strengthen our faith, and
keep us close to You. In Jesus' name we ask it. Amen. (28)

Caring for a Dying Loved One

O God, my loved one is nearing the time of death. Help me to speak words of assurance to him (her) as well as to provide caring comfort that will help him (her) to rest well. He (she) has been my companion for many years and has been a blessing and inspiration to me. I am glad that he (she) knows You and Your saving grace through Your Son, Jesus Christ. I take comfort in the Scripture verse that promises, "He who raised the Lord Jesus will raise us also with Jesus" (2 Corinthians 4:14). Amen. (29)

For a Blessed End

O dear God and Lord! I live, yet I know not how long. I must die and yet I do not know when. But as You alone know, then O Lord, my heavenly Father let it be so! Should this day [this night] be the last of my life, Lord, Your will be done, for it alone is the best way. Therefore, I am ready to live and die in true faith in Christ, my Redeemer. Yet grant me but this plea, that I do not die suddenly in my sins. Give me a properly created knowledge, repentance, and sorrow concerning the sins that I have committed. Show them clearly to me in this life, that they might not be shown clearly on the Day of Judgment, and that because of that, I would go forth to everlasting shame before the sight of angels and of all people. O merciful Father, do not forsake me and take not Your Holy Spirit from me. Give me enough time and space for repentance that I may acknowledge and confess the transgressions of my heart, that I may obtain forgiveness and comfort from your saving Word, and that I may be preserved for eternal life. O Lord, who knows all hearts, my heart yearns for its future with You, let me die when You so will. Yet, insofar that it is possible, grant me a reasonable, quiet, and blessed end.

O God, be gracious and merciful to me, a poor sinner. Amen. (30)

> Lord Jesus Christ, the highest good,
> You I implore through Your dear blood,
> Just make my final hour good!

For the Sick and For the Dying

Lord God, heavenly Father, look with favor upon this Your redeemed child, forgive him (her) all his (her) sin, comfort him (her) with the promise of resurrection to life everlasting; through Jesus Christ, Your Son, our Lord. Amen. (31)

For Trust in God

You alone, O Lord, make the decision of life and death, reminding us that You are the one who holds our life in Your hands. By this knowledge teach us holy fear of You, to repent of our sin, and to worship You in humble trust. But especially make known to us through Your servants the meritorious sufferings and death of Your Son, Jesus Christ, by whom the effect of death is cancelled. You take away, O Lord, because of our sin, but You give life because of Christ. Blessed be Your name. Keep us ever confident in Jesus through our Baptism and His holy body and blood, that we may depart this vale of tears and enter into Your heavenly kingdom. Amen. (32)

Medical Professionals

O Lord Jesus Christ, who has power of life and death, of health and of sickness, give power, wisdom, and gentleness to all Your ministering spirits: all physicians and surgeons, nurses and watchers of the sick, that, always bearing Your presence with them, they may not only heal but bless and shine as lamps of hope in the darkest hours of distress and fear; through Jesus Christ, Your Son, our Lord. Amen. (33)

Medical Professionals

Most merciful Father, You have committed to our love and care our fellow human beings and their necessities. Graciously be with and prosper all those who serve the sick and those in need. Let their service be abundantly blessed as they bring relief to the suffering, comfort to the sorrowing, and peace to the dying. Grant them the knowledge that inasmuch as they do it unto the least of the Master's brethren, they do it unto Him; through the same Jesus Christ, our Lord. (34)

Peace at Life's End

God, who made the earth and heaven, Darkness and light: You the day for work have given, For rest the night. May Your angel guards defend us, Slumber sweet Your mercy send us, Holy dreams and hopes attend us All through the night.

And when morn again shall call us To run life's way, May we still, whate'er befall us, Your will obey. From the pow'r of evil hide us, In the narrow pathway guide us, Never be Your smile denied us All through the day.

Guard us waking, guard us sleeping, And when we die, May we in Your mighty keeping All peaceful lie. When the last dread call shall wake us, Then, O Lord, do not forsake us, But to reign in glory take us With You on high. Amen. (*LSB* 877:1–3) (35)

Nunc Dimittis (Lord, Now You Let)

Lord, now You let Your servant go in peace; Your word has been fulfilled. My own eyes have seen the salvation which You have prepared in the sight of ev'ry people: A light to reveal You to the nations and the glory of Your people Israel. Glory be to the Father and to the Son and to the Holy Spirit; as it was in the beginning, is now, and will be forever. Amen. (*LSB*, p. 165) (36)

For the Sick and For the Dying

Depart in peace, you ransomed soul. May God the Father almighty who created you; may God the Son who redeemed you with His blood, may God the Holy Spirit who sanctified you in the water of Holy Baptism, receive you into the company of the saints and angels who live in the light of His glory forevermore; through Jesus Christ, Your Son, our Lord. Amen. (37)

Steadfast Trust

Increase my faith, dear Savior, For Satan seeks by night and day To rob me of this treasure And take my hope of bliss away. But, Lord, with You beside me, I shall be undismayed; And led by Your good Spirit, I shall be unafraid. Abide with me, O Savior, A firmer faith bestow; Then I shall bid defiance To ev'ry evil foe.

In faith, Lord, let me serve You; Though persecution, grief, and pain Should seek to overwhelm me, Let me a steadfast trust retain; And then at my departure, Lord, take me home to You, Your riches to inherit As all You said holds true. In life and death, Lord, keep me Until Your heav'n I gain, Where I by Your great mercy The end of faith attain. Amen. (*LSB* 587:2, 3) (38)

For a Blessed End

Merciful and gracious God, I perceive that the time of my departure is near, that I shall depart in peace and lie down to rest. My sight fails me, my strength is leaving me, and it seems as if my change is at hand. So I come to You and offer my last prayer, which is this: I commend my spirit to You, O Lord, and ask for a blessed end through Jesus Christ! Amen.

Lord God, heavenly Father, You have created me and have always provided for me and sustained me. Now, mercifully receive my soul. O Jesus, You have redeemed and washed me with Your blood. Now let me die saved in true faith, trusting in Your merit and blood. O Lord Jesus, into Your hands I commend my spirit. O precious Holy Spirit, my comforter and aid, do not forsake me now. Give me courage and the assurance that I am an heir of everlasting life. Pray in me and with me, and make intercession for me before God with groans too deep for words.

Behold, I am ready to leave this earth, and am longing only for You and to be with You, most Blessed Trinity! As the children of Israel had their Year of Jubilee, when every slave was liberated and all property was restored, so, O my God, my year of jubilee begins when I die, and delivered from the service of every sin and the burden of every cross, I attain to the perfect liberty of the children of God in the life everlasting.

O my Jesus, open to me the door of heaven, accompany and guide me to everlasting life, to the congregation of the saints in light. O my God, grant me a rational end, that

I may keep my mind to the last moment of my life. Keep me in holy and good thoughts, that I may ever remember Jesus Christ. And if my eyes should grow dim, refresh my soul inwardly with Your heavenly comfort and light. Let Jesus ever stand before the eyes of my soul. Grant that I may rejoice in the blood that He shed for me, and that I may hide myself in His pierced side, take comfort in His merit, and by true faith lay hold of His righteousness.

If it pleases You, grant me a gentle death. Preserve me from impatient actions, temptations, and distracting thoughts. Let my heart, which has been Your dwelling here, gently throb its last. Let me die calmly in Your arms. Grant me a blessed end, that I may soon behold Your holy countenance with rejoicing.

O Blessed Trinity, bless my going out from this present mortality and my coming into happy eternity. The Lord bless me and keep me; the Lord make His face to shine upon me and be gracious to me; the Lord lift up His countenance upon me and give me peace! In the name of the triune God, the Father, Son, and Holy Spirit, I live and I die. In His name I close my eyes and commit myself to God and His mercy.

Let me depart this life Confiding in my Savior; By grace receive my soul That it may live forever; And let my body have A quiet resting place Within a Christian grave; And let it sleep in peace. Amen. (*LSB* 696:5) (39)

Brief Order of Prayer

Leader: In the name of the Father and of the Son and of the Holy Spirit.

All: Amen.

All: Lord, have mercy. Christ, have mercy. Lord, have mercy.

A PSALM may be read by the leader or by the family in response.

All: Glory be to the Father and to the Son and to the Holy Spirit; as it was in the beginning, is now, and will be forever. Amen.

THE SCRIPTURE READING
THE MEDITATION THE PRAYER
THE LORD'S PRAYER

Leader: Let us bless the Lord.
All: Thanks be to God.

Leader: The almighty and merciful God, the Father, the Son, and the Holy Spirit, bless us and keep us.
All: Amen.

Index of Sources

Meditations

Meditations 1, 5, 6, 7, 18, and 20 are from Richard Andersen, *For Grieving Friends*. St. Louis: Concordia, 1975.

Meditations 2 and 8 are from Donald L. Deffner, *At the Death of a Child: Words of Comfort and Hope*. St. Louis: Concordia, 1993.

Meditation 3 is from Donald L. Deffner, *At Life's End: Words of Comfort and Hope*. St. Louis: Concordia, 1995.

Meditations 4, 9, 15, 16, and 32 are from *Sermons for Funerals, Weddings and Civil Holidays: Selections from Concordia Pulpit Resources*. St. Louis: Concordia, 2008.

Meditations 10, 11, 17, 23, 28, 29, 30, 31, 33, and 35 are from Arthur A. Just Jr. and Scot A. Kinnaman, *Visitation: Resources for the Care of Souls*. St. Louis: Concordia, 2008.

Meditations 12, 13, and 14 are from Bryan Wolfmueller, *Final Victory: Contemplating the Death and Funeral of a Christian*. St. Louis: Concordia, 2010.

Meditation 19 is from Johann Gerhard, *Gerhard's Sacred Meditations*. Translated by Rev. Charles W. Heisler. Philadelphia: Lutheran Publication Society, 1896.

Meditation 21 is from *Portals of Prayer*. St. Louis: Concordia, August 4, 1940.

Meditation 22 is from Barry J. Keurulainen, *Walking in the Shadows: A Study of Death and Grief*. St. Louis: Concordia, 1992.

Meditations 24, 25, 26, and 27 are from James C. Galvin, ed. *Through Faith Alone: 365 Devotional Readings from Martin Luther*.

Meditation 34 is from *Starck's Prayer Book*. St. Louis: Concordia, 2009.

Prayers

Prayers 1, 3, 11, 16, 17, and 29 are adapted from *Blessings and Prayers for Caregivers*, Annetta Dellinger and Karen Boerger. St. Louis: Concordia, 2010.

Prayers 2, 21, 22, 26, 28, and 30 are taken from *Lutheran Book of Prayer*. St. Louis: Concordia, 2005.

Prayers 6, 18, 20, 31, and 33 are adapted from *The Daily Office*, Herbert Lindemann, ed. St. Louis: Concordia, 1965.

Prayer 8 is taken from *Blessings and Prayers for Women*. St. Louis: Concordia, 2004.

Prayer 10 is taken from *Portals of Prayer*. St. Louis: Concordia, January–March 2009.

Prayers 12, 15, and 24 are adapted from the tract *Prayers in Bereavement*. St. Louis: Concordia, n.d.

Prayer 14 is taken from *Lutheran Worship: Little Agenda*. St. Louis: Concordia, 1985.

Prayer 19 is taken from *Portals of Prayer*. St. Louis: Concordia, October–December 2009.

Prayer 23 is taken from *Final Victory: Contemplating the Death and Funeral of a Christian*. St. Louis: Concordia, 2009.

Prayers 25 and 34 are taken from *Lutheran Worship: Altar Book*. St. Louis: Concordia, 1984.

Prayers 27, 35, 36, and 38 are taken from *Lutheran Service Book*. St. Louis: Concordia, 2006.

Prayer 37 is taken from *Lutheran Worship: Agenda*. St. Louis: Concordia, 1984.

Prayer 32 is from Arthur A. Just Jr. and Scot A. Kinnaman, *Visitation: Resources for the Care of Souls*. St. Louis: Concordia, 2008.

Prayer 39 is from *Starck's Prayer Book*. St. Louis: Concordia, 2009.

Prayers not specified above are written for this edition by the editor, for Concordia Publishing House.

Other

"Time for Prayer" is from Arthur A. Just Jr. and Scot A. Kinnaman, *Visitation: Resources for the Care of Souls*. St. Louis: Concordia, 2008.

"Life, Death, and the Resurrection" and "Grief: What to Expect" are from Bryan Wolfmueller, *Final Victory: Contemplating the Death and Funeral of a Christian*. St. Louis: Concordia, 2009.

Topical Index of Meditations